Endorsements

"*What an awakening message!*–I got as much out of *Unleash Your Significance* as I have from books written by *Joel Goldsmith, Wayne Dyer and Iyanla Vanzant.* It is lovingly written as Catrice soulfully shares personal experiences that pushed her into self-reflection, growth and healing. She candidly shares valuable ways to break through the inner barriers that stunt our ability to flourish and provides real strategies to help us move past our personal paralysis. This book should be required reading for everyone in all the professional schools primarily for the life preparation and healing properties it provides."

— Robin Tillotson–CEO/Chief Cultural Officer | This I Do For Me

"Catrice shares an eye-opening message on discovering your life purpose and unleashing one's significance into the world. Her thought provoking questions allows the reader to apply a self-examination, in order to get to the bottom of where they currently are in life. Her transparency about her personal journey allows the reader to easily identify with her struggles and successes. She empowers the reader to know their worth and helps them to recognize their significance!"

— Felicia Lucas, CEO of His Glory Creations

"I am a true believer that everyone has greatness inside of them – that we all exist to fulfill something unique in the earth. The dash between our birth date and death date should have significance. The world should know that we were here by the impact that we had. With that, this book is in perfect alignment with what God is doing in this season. It's time for the masses to unleash their significance. No more hiding in the bleachers, it is time for us all to step on our stage, whatever that stage looks like, and be who He has called us to be. I encourage you to get the book and take action. Your destiny awaits, come on let's do this!"

— Anita Clinton, Minister, Author & Speaker, Be Great Ministries

"Making life changes can be tough. There is no time for self-doubt, blame or regret. Her relevant, insightful and inspirational message will shake you up and empower you to transform your life. Catrice's sense of humor and straight talk is refreshing and reads like having a conversation with a close friend. She helps you recognize that living out your destiny is what's next for you!"

— Dana Mallon, Trauma Recovery Strategist, Soulfit Women

"Understanding and embracing your purpose is one of the most self-actualizing aspects of living. If you are ready to Unleash your Significance the exercises and content help you identify, acknowledge, embrace, and cultivate your life's purpose so that you can truly start living. This book will open your ears so you can hear the divine whispering of your purpose and open your heart so you can accept it. Unleash Your Significance is engaging, empowering and timely."

— Dr. Eboni Ivory Green, Co-Founder Caregiver Support Services

UNLEASH
YOUR SIGNIFICANCE

Activate the Audacity to Be All You Are Destined to Be

Catrice M. Jackson, M.S., LMHP, LPC

Catriceology Enterprises

Published by Catriceology Enterprises
Omaha, NE | United States of America

FOR INFORMATION CONTACT:
Catrice M. Jackson, M.S., LMHP, LPC
Global Visionary Leader of the Awakened Conscious Shift, International Speaker, BOSSLady of Branding and International Best-Selling Author

Online ordering is available for all products.
www.catriceology.com
www.bossladyofbranding.com
www.catriceologyenterprises.com

ISBN-13: 978-0983839842 (Catriceology Enterprises)
ISBN-10: 0983839840

Book Cover Design: *Ozone Media Group*
Editor: *Renee Dabney | The Write Bud*
Interior Design: *Tieshena Davis | Purposely Created Publishing*

Printed in the USA
10 9 8 7 6 5 4 3 2

Dedication

For Tahsahn and Tyson

When your heart stops and you cannot breathe any more, this is the end of life as you know it. When you take your last breath, above all else, what matters most are the people you love and moments you shared with them.

This book is dedicated to my heart beat and my breath: my grandson, my son... my *legacy*. It is for them I live. They inspire me every day to be a better woman, mother, grandmother, leader, human being, and legacy builder. When I take my last breath, I want them to have a piece of me that still lives... my soul, my voice, my message and my vision.

Tahsahn and Tyson, never forget you are Sons of the Almighty Father, Kings among Kings and heir to God's throne. You lack nothing! There is greatness within you. Never forget that. You are powerful beyond measure and salt and light in the world. You are worthy. You matter. You are magnificently, significant!

Daringly and unapologetically unleash *your* significance, own your King status and courageously walk in your greatness all the days of your life. Rise up and take your place in the world as men of God, fathers of love, gladiators of greatness and leaders for the Kingdom.

I love you and thank you for loving me unconditionally. I AM grateful and blessed. With every breath you take and every step you make always remember this...

"I can do all things through Christ which strengthen me." – Philippians 4:13

THANKS MOM

To my mother, Robbie Jackson, I'm blessed to call you mom. Because of the woman you are, I am the woman I AM. Thank you for modeling love, courage, tenacity, resiliency, obedience, faith and sacrifice. When life became difficult, these traits carried me through and over the obstacles. Thank you for being a woman of tenacity, resourcefulness and faith.

Preface

There is *not one* human being on this entire planet that has it *all* together. Not one person who knows it all and not one who doesn't have any struggles in their life at this very moment. – Not a single person in the world!

Even the people who "appear" to have it all and know it all, fall short, fail in one capacity or another, feel defeated at times and worry about what the future holds for them. It's very common for us as human beings to excel in one area of our lives and struggle in others. It's also normal for us to look at other people's lives and careers and wish we were them or desire the wisdom they used to create the success and fulfillment they experience. It's human for us to wonder how some people just seem to know it all, have it all and have it all together.

We are voyeuristic people. By nature, we are people watchers, observers of behavior, and, let's keep it real, coveters of other people' lives, possessions and wealth. Sadly, for us, our instinctual desire to compare, judge and compete with our fellow humans causes a great deal of unnecessary stress and self-abuse. Theodore Roosevelt says it best, "*Comparison is the thief of joy.*"

You may think your biggest saboteurs are other people; they are not. *You* are responsible for where you are at this time in your life and where you'll end up. This truth is bittersweet. It may take some time for you to digest it, but, the sooner you do, get busy taking responsibility for creating the life of your dreams, the better and happier you will be.

Have you ever witnessed someone become a star "over night" or all of a sudden have a miraculous breakthrough in their business and soar to the top? Have you ever thought *how can I help others be successful in their business when your business is not successful*? Have you ever coveted another person's relationships, wealth or material things? I have, and nine times out of ten, after peeking through the windows of their life, it made me feel miserable because I was comparing my life to theirs.

I wrote this book to help you stop self-abusing and to remind you of how *magnificent* you truly are! I wrote this book to help you remember you are one of the greats, just like the ones you may admire. I wrote this book to affirm your divine existence in the world. I wrote this book to inspire you to have the faith, belief and the audacity to remember your purpose and *Unleash Your Significance* unapologetically in the world. *You matter. You have value. There is no one like you in the world, and that is powerful beyond measure. You're here for a special assignment. You are significant!*

This is your moment to walk in your majestic greatness! This is your moment to *believe* in your awesomeness and audaciously create and live a life that is meaningful, one that matters and one where you make a difference in the lives of other people. This is your destiny! I don't know what the future holds for you or me, but, I know we are responsible for how we live in the *dash;* the precious moment of life we create between birth and death. *Who are you going to be? How are you going to live? What will you experience? How will you use your gifts to serve the world?*

This is the moment you say *"no more"* to just letting life happen to you. This is your moment to choose how you will live out your destiny dash. If you took your last breath tomorrow… would you have fulfilled your destiny? Don't wait any longer. Tomorrow is not promised. I know you have hopes, dreams and desires; now is the time to fulfill and live *every* single one of them.

Your destiny is waiting for you! It's time for you to show up, say "yes" to it and live it full out. *I don't know it all. I don't have it all. I don't have it all together.* I'm on my destiny journey too. Let's walk it out together!

Introduction

Hello Magnificent One!

I've been waiting for you…

You see… I know you've been on *"The Journey."* – And, I know with every courageous step, you've been on the roller coaster ride of your life! You've anxiously held your breath on the uncertain trek to the top. You've beamed with joy and pride as you reached the sometimes elusive summit. And, you've hollered like there was no tomorrow on the terrifying descent to the bottom.

And then… you strap back in, not knowing exactly what to expect… to experience it all again.

Over and over, again, you say *"yes"* to the unpredictable, splendid, agonizing, wondrous, journey called life. One minute you're riding the heart-wrenching roller coaster, and, in the next moment, you're on easy street going with subtle ebbs and flows of the Merry-Go-Round. Back and forth between the two predictable extremes… this is how you're living out your dash.

You are trapped in the *Life Happens Amusement Park*. The clowns in your life are acting a fool. Life is playing impossible games on you that you just can't seem to win. You know there's got to be more than the smoke and mirrors and the expected craziness of the carnival.

Well here's the truth.

You are born. You live. You die. – This is the final destination for you. You have no choice in this undesirable ultimate ending. It's destiny.

But... you *do* have a choice in how you fulfill your *living* destiny! You have the *power to choose* who you want to be, what you want to do and what you want to experience in the *dash*, the precious time between *life* — and — *death*.

I invite you to *choose* how your living destiny *will* be fulfilled. — It's time for an alternative experience; One that's remarkable and life-changing!

Here's your invitation...

Come with me on a *soul journey* to remember what you've forgotten.

Say "yes" to my invitation to forever leave the *"Life Happens Amusement Park,"* and embark on an inspirational adventure to ignite what you *deserve*, *desire* and *dream* about.

Say "yes" to the most thrilling and fulfilling part of the journey by... *Unleashing Your Significance!*

There's so much more to what you perceive as your life. There's something marvelous outside the confines of the amusement park you've existed in. — I don't know what you've been through, what you're going through or where you're headed, but I invite you to take a detour to discover your destiny.

What you see in your life right now is NOT your destiny. It's not the final outcome! — Unless you BELIEVE it is all it will be and all that you deserve.

You may not have it all or have it all together. It may look like you'll never get ahead. It may look like the world is against you. It may look like your turn is never going to come. It may not look like your work is producing a harvest.

I love what Wayne Dyer says, *"When you change the way you look at things, things will change."*

There's clarity in your chaos — look for it.
There's beauty in your ashes — look for it.

There's power in your problems — look for it.
There's light in your darkness — look for it.

Do not despise where you are (or who you are) right now. It's all preparation for your *purpose*. It's a part of your destiny plan!

I know you've been striving for success. Winning sometimes and feeling utterly defeated other times. I know you've been chasing cash and in hot pursuit of big pay days and promotions. And, I know there have been moments that you've been tired, frustrated and overwhelmed more times than you can count every step of the way. Success is a wonderful experience and great accomplishment, but there's something more nourishing for you to experience...

There's more for you. There's more for you to be, do and have.

Today, I invite you to step outside of the perspective that life is just happening to you and into a panoramic view of what's limitlessly possible.

There's a bigger purpose for your life. There's undeniable greatness within you! There's something magnificent for you to do in the world. You matter. You have value. You're here for a special reason; a divine assignment only you can complete. *Your destiny is waiting for you*!

There's no more time to waste! You don't need permission or approval. It's your life, and it's 100% up to you, how you live it. What will the legacy of your life dash be? How will you be remembered? What mark are you going to leave in the world?

One day you'll take your last breath without warning. Who are you going to be, and how will you live in the dash between life and death?

Come on this journey with me to unshackle your greatness, re-discover your purpose, **Unleash Your Significance and Be All You Are Destined to Be.**

Let's go! Lace up your destiny shoes, be audacious and let's create some meaningful magic!

UNLEASH
YOUR **SIGNIFICANCE**

Activate the Audacity to Be All You Are Destined to Be

Table of Contents

" The key to realizing a dream is to focus not on success, but on significance, and then, even the small steps and little victories along your path will take on greater meaning."

— Oprah Winfrey

CHAPTER ONE

"We do not see things as they are; we

see things as we are."

— Anais Nin

Chapter 1
Your Destiny Is In the Dash

ACTIVATE CLARITY

"The two most important days in your life are the day you are born and the day you find out why." – Mark Twain

THIS IS IT! It's time. Your last beautiful breath is moments away. With every exhale, you feel what you've known as your *life* becoming a distant memory. This moment, the pinnacle of life as you lived it will be no more in just a few more seconds. Time has run out. There will be no tomorrow. You will never feel the touch of your cherished ones' embrace. You've had your last laugh. Your fears and worries will all be over soon. This is the end of your living journey.

You'll never dance another dance, sing another song, or cry another tear. Faintly, yet distinctly, you hear your name being called. You hear the sweet whisper of your creator's voice lovingly beckoning you to let go to be intimately in his presence. The precious inhale of breath lessens as you linger between the spaces of here and there. This is it. Your time in your beloved body is over! There is no more you and life as you know it. At last... you've taken your last breath.

Have you lived the life you were destined to live? Did you fulfill your purpose? Did you dance with your destiny? Did you *really* live? Did you take the expensive trip, savor the decadent cake, love unconditionally and fully express the beauty of your soul? Or did you accept what life dished out to you? Were you stingy with your love and affection? Did you guard your wounded heart and never fully experience soulful love? Was your life full of anger, frustration, regret and fear? How much energy did you waste on worrying about what other people thought of you or how much time did you let pass, by fearing failure and being afraid of success?

There are no second chances. This is it! You have one life to live. You were born. And you will die; but how you live in the *dash* between life and death is up to you, and only you. Are you *allowing* life to happen *to* you, or are you creating the moments leading to the fulfillment of your unique destiny? There was a time in my younger years that I believed life was *happening to me instead of for me*. I spent way too many days to count being angry and frustrated with life, with other people and with myself. I've been sad and mad about how people in my past talked about me, treated me, left and abandoned me, chose others over me, left me out, took me for granted, and misused my love, loyalty and generosity. I've blamed them for my past circumstances and held grudges far too long. And then, I shamed myself by falsely believing there must be something *wrong* with *me* that other people would want to treat me this way.

There used to be moments where I thought I was not *pretty* enough, not *smart* enough, not *skinny* enough and not *worthy* enough. As much as I hate to admit it, I had *chosen* to be a **victim** in life even though the word *victim* was a word I never thought I would ever be. I mean come on, who in their "right mind" would *choose* to be a victim? Truthfully, you, me and every other human being you know has *chosen* to be a victim (of our own self-abuse) at least once in their life. By victim, I mean *allowing* life to just happen instead of creating the life and life experiences we want. What a disempowering place to be in when we allow other people's opinions of us or their actions towards us to determine how we feel about ourselves.

Yes, I know we cannot control how other people treat us, but we are 100% in control of how we respond or whether or not we are going to *believe* the direct or indirect message behind their actions. While I didn't self-abuse, (allow other's actions to paralyze me) too often, it happened. And although I don't currently feel the pain, I remember most of the moments pretty clearly. I can honestly say that 98% of my past wounds are completely healed. I carry no grudges or resentment towards anyone who has hurt, wounded, or abandoned me in the past.

> I have deeply forgiven my teachers. Yes, they *all* were teachers in some kind of way. You know how the saying goes, *"people come into your life for a reason, a season or a lifetime."* My teachers came into my life to teach me something about life, love and myself. Ultimately, I believe they all came to teach me about *my* significance!

Our teachers, those who we share moments with during life's journey, come to evoke only two emotions: love or fear and often times both. Every day we experience variations of love or fear on a continuum of emotions. Emotions such as horror, pain, sadness, grief, doubt, jealousy, envy, and anger are different expressions of fear. Emotions such as joy, peace, excitement, pleasure, and or happiness are expressions of love. *And every expression is a choice.* We can choose to be happy despite our circumstances, or we can choose to be sad because of our circumstances.

No one *makes* us feel any certain way. **We choose it**. Our teachers help us make the choice. Perhaps the girl or boy who bullied you when you were in elementary school came into your life to teach you how to find your strength. Maybe the best friend who betrayed you came to teach you how to be more discerning or to trust after pain. If you're honest and look closely, you'll see the important lessons they came to *teach* you.

Do you feel like you are repeating the same lessons over and over again? Does it seem like the same teachers keep showing up repeatedly? If your teachers continue to deliver lessons in the variations of fear, there's a reason. And, if you find yourself frequently saying *"why me or why is this happening again,"* you haven't completed the lesson or passed the test. So a new teacher shows up with the same lesson delivered in a different way. If you're tired of feeling doubtful, you must start believing in yourself and stop willingly taking a front row seat in the classroom of despair. Unconsciously, you choose teachers who will either confirm or deny what you already believe to be true about you.

Imagine attending a University for the first time. Your advisor instructs you to honestly choose one class for the next semester. You're told to walk down the hall, take a left and you'll see two classrooms to choose from. On one door the sign says *"The Genius Club"* and the other door's sign says *"The Average Academy."* Which door would you choose? Do you believe deep down inside that you are average, ordinary, just a regular person? Or do you in your soul *know* you are indeed a genius, above average, an extraordinary human being? This is *not* the time to let your ego takeover. This is the time to tell the truth about how you *really* feel about yourself in this very moment. There is no right or wrong answer here. The best answer will be a truthful answer. *Who do you believe you are*?

You see, who you believe you are determines what you believe you deserve. And what you believe you deserve, you unconsciously attract into your life. And many times, that which you attract also comes in the form of teachers and experiences with a uniquely coded *soul lesson* built in just for you. Now let me clarify this. I am totally against people harming people. I do NOT condone any type of violence or abuse towards anyone. And, I despise all intentional pain people choose to inflict upon another human being.

I know you've been through some things. I know people have intentionally and unintentionally hurt or abused you. I know some of those wounds are still gaping with throbbing pain and quiet despair. And NO, you did NOT *deserve* whatever abuse anyone has inflicted upon you. That's not the kind of "deserve" I'm talking about. What I'm clearly saying is, when you have *unconscious beliefs* that *"you are not worthy, you are unlovable, you are not enough, and or you don't matter"* – when you experience unpleasant things, on a deep unconscious level you believe somehow you deserved it.

Whoever has hurt you in the past (or who is hurting you right now) is 100% responsible for the infliction. YOU, however, are 100% responsible for how you respond to it, whether you walk away or not, and or whether you internalize their behavior as truth about who you are. All of this is up to you; *it's a choice.* If you want to change your circumstances, you must change your choices. Every decision to change takes you one step closer to your dreams and destiny.

Today, I'm challenging you to *believe you are worthy*. Today, I'm challenging you to *forgive those unpleasant and abusive teachers*. Today, I'm challenging you to *be courageous regardless of your circumstances*. And today, I'm challenging you to *be 100% responsible for how you choose to live in the dash*. It's your dash! Don't let other people steal your dreams or derail your destiny. How will you choose to live out your dash?

We've been conditioned, programmed and groomed by society to relentlessly pursue success at all cost beginning with our first outside of the womb breath. Our parents have encouraged us to talk, crawl, walk and run with cheers of *you can do it*! Once we left home and entered the school system, the programming continued with concepts such as grading scales, pass or fail tests, achievement scores and entrance exams. Test after test we leaped, jumped, and hurdled over our challenges to "become" successful. And, if that wasn't enough, we took success into our own hands by setting off on our own adult journey to live the *idealized dream* we had been programmed to believe was the *perfect* picture of success.

In hot pursuit, we enrolled in college, went into the Armed Forces, started technical training programs and or started our own families, all with one thing in mind: to achieve our personal goals and *become successful*. College, degrees, higher education, training, workshops, certificates, awards, promotions, marriage, parenthood, good jobs, nice homes and fancy cars, all of it intentionally and unconsciously programmed into every fiber of our being. We've been conditioned by society, parents and friends to *by any means necessary* BE successful.

What does that mean anyway? **Success** according to the dictionary means *"the fact of getting or achieving wealth, respect or fame."* Additionally, it means *"the correct or desired result of an attempt or outcome."* So, essentially by these definitions, success means becoming wealthy, earning respect, becoming famous and getting what we want.

Well no wonder so many people are sad, struggling, stuck and unsatisfied in life! Success tells us and requires us to pursue external results in order to be happy and satisfied on the inside. Success tells us to get high scores, pass the tests, get the promotions, win the big game, invest in real estate, take out loans, get the big house and go into debt on the path to pursuing our dreams. Success dictates we make sacrifices, work extra hours, stay up late to study, prolong relationships and having children, and do whatever it takes to *prove* we are successful.

Did I do any of the above? I sure did! Did I become successful? Yes, I did. Do I regret doing any of it? Generally speaking, no I do not regret the achievements I've accomplished over the years. I don't regret the ultimate outcome, yet, I must admit the time spent getting to the "destination" could have been spent in more *meaningful* ways. Here's why I say this. I believe *we all are born on purpose with a purpose.* I believe we come into this life with innate skills, talents and spiritual gifts. When I say spiritual gifts, I mean natural talents and skill sets that require no education, degrees, certifications, exams or special training. Some people call it purpose, and others may refer to it as a *calling*. I use both of those words interchangeably, yet, I prefer to use the term *gifts*; *divine gifts* that only God gives us to carry out our special divine assignment in the world.

I can recall at a very young age that I had five *divine gifts* in particular. Those gifts are sensing, feeling, knowing (intuition), teaching and speaking. For as long as I can remember, I just seemed to know certain things. Although I often didn't say anything, I had the uncanny ability to *know* in my spirit what other people were thinking and feeling. I could feel and sense when others were sad, angry or disappointed. People watching and interpreting the behaviors of others came naturally, and I've been fascinated by how people show up in the world and behave. I didn't fully understand the power of these gifts back then, but, as time passed, it became clear how I would use them in my future work.

Maybe you've heard of this technique sometimes used to help people discover their purpose. It's been said that, if you can think back to the age of seven or eight and remember what you *really loved* doing, you can find traces of your purpose in the world. I believe there is great truth in that concept. What did you absolutely love doing at seven or eight? What did you do naturally that you could do all day without getting bored? What were you good at that made you feel happy or alive inside? Can you remember that far back? I can.

I loved to play school, and I'll admit I had to be the teacher. Playing school wasn't fun unless I was in front of the class (even if there was only one student) leading and teaching. I didn't have aspirations to be a real school teacher, but, over the years, I discovered I loved being in front of people. I enjoyed talking, teaching, educating and empowering others. Eventually I went on to sing after discovering I had *a voice.* I participated in school talent shows, sung in the school and church choir, took speech classes and seized every opportunity to use my voice.

Shortly before I became pregnant with my only child, back in the early 1990's, I had a dream of going on the show *Star Search.* You may not remember it, but it was one of the first singing competition shows on television. My first BIG dream was to be a famous singer and recording artist. I had my little demo tape ready (on cassette tape) and had actually written my first song titled, *"Where Is the Love."* Yeah, that was a time in my life when I was searching for someone (a man) to love me unconditionally. Nevertheless, within a year, I found out I was pregnant with a son, and that dream quickly faded into the background of my life. I didn't get the opportunity to take the big stage, but I was blessed with a man-child who gave me all the unconditional love I could stand.

Before I graduated from high school, I knew my voice was my greatest divine gift and that my place in the world was on the platform. I was born to teach, speak, empower and lead others through the power of my voice. I didn't know why or how I was going to do it, but, I knew the divine skills of sensing, feeling, knowing, feeling, teaching and speaking would be essential in living out my destiny. I was clear on the "what" (what my gifts were) but, I was unclear on the "how" (how I was going to manifest my destiny), the "why"

(why God chose me for this purpose) and "when" (when the purpose would become clear) most of my twenties and thirties.

> *Can you relate to this? Do you know you have special talents and skills, but because you are unclear about the details, you feel like your life is on pause or has taken a detour? Do you doubt your genius and brilliance, and are you delaying your destiny?*

Here's what I need you to understand clearly. *All of it matters!* Every heartbreak, pain, struggle, triumph, victory, loss, gain, obstacle, opportunity... I mean *everything* you've experienced thus far *matters*. It's all shaping and molding you into the person you need to become in order to fulfill your destiny and be significant in the world. You may not understand it all. You may not know the how, why, or when, but, if you know the what, your destiny is *choices* away from being fulfilled. If you want to have a panoramic view of your purpose for living, you've got to step out of your story and view it as an observer. You got to get out of the middle of the madness and go to the outer parameters of your life. You must see your life from the perspective that God sees it. *Your purpose is not in the pieces of your life; it's in the whole.*

It's so easy to get caught up in your circumstances. It's easy to be in a situation that sucks and that's all you can see. It thoroughly sucks to be living moment by moment and not clearly know who you are and what you are here to divinely accomplish in your life time. What is worse than that? It's unsettling to be successful and not know your true greatness. It's bothersome to not know what being significant in the world is. It's disheartening to one day look at all of your successes and accomplishments and still not be deeply fulfilled. I know because I've been there.

> *You'll never feel like you are on the path to your purpose and destiny if you keep dissecting every moment and experience to discover why.*

I want you to do something very powerful today. I want you to be brave enough to say YES to a panoramic view of your life purpose. I want you to step outside of where you are right now and *view your life like an observer instead of a participant.* Right now you are smack dab in the center of your circumstances. You can't see the forest because of the trees. You are the main actor, and you cannot see the performance because you are performing it. You can't see the beauty in the brokenness. You can't see the power in the pain. You can't see the glory in the gloom. You can't see that *everything* happening to you right now is happening for your greater good. I know it's hard to do sometimes, but you *must* step outside of what you see because where you ARE is NOT your destiny!

So how do you get the panoramic view? *You step out of the center of your life.* This means you stop being selfish. Life is not just about you. While you may be wallowing in pity, the people you're meant to serve are waiting for you to show up. The mess you may be in needs to be translated into a message that will set others free. While your purpose may include you, it is NOT about you. The question to ask yourself in this moment is, *"how is what I'm going through right now meant to help me serve the world?"* Unleashing the answer to this question will help you step outside of your circumstances and see the bigger picture of your purpose.

Your view becomes panoramic when you step away from events, places and spaces that hinder your purpose. What groups, clubs, networks or organizations do you belong to that are full of more drama than dream strategies and destiny conversations? If you are tired of your circumstances, check your circle. In order to make your dreams come true, you have to hang out with destiny seekers not dream doubters. You'll never fully live out your purpose if you hang out with people who have a pessimistic perspective. These kinds of people see problems instead of possibilities. They would rather talk about obstacles than take advantage of opportunities.

What's more important than checking your circle is checking yourself! Are YOU the one who talks more about your drama than your dreams? Are you pessimistic and all you can see are your problems? Are you too busy wallowing in your obstacles versus seeing them as opportunities to expand your greatness? Are you too busy reliving the pain to pursue the possibilities right in front of you? If you ARE the *problem,* you are *existing and not living* and definitely NOT living on purpose. You must expand your view!

Your view becomes panoramic when you step away from people who are blocking your blessings. Who are the people in your life who do not encourage or support you? Who are the people who put you down instead of lifting you up? Who are the people in your life that don't want you to grow, transform, or succeed? I KNOW you know who they are. The better question to ask is *why* are you allowing them to remain in your life? This is where *what you believe* about yourself comes into play. This is where your deserve level comes into play. Why do you believe you deserve their toxic presence on your life?

I know some of them are family members, and you feel like you must keep them in your life. That may be partially true. You may not be able to remove them permanently, but, YOU CAN put them on the parameter of your life. Stop allowing people to sit on your couch and sleep in your bed when you have the power and choice to put them in the attic or in the basement. And some you may need to put in the garage or on the curb. You may not be able to totally walk away, but you don't have to invite them into your home and offer them a meal and a place to stay. *It's always your choice!*

Just because you experience both pain and glory in your life does not mean you do not have greatness within you. Just because you are experiencing problems does not mean there isn't a significance purpose for your life. *What are you doing with your dash*? It's your life and how you live *your dash* is totally up to you. It's time to shift your focus. I've witnessed many people who put too much energy into being petty, pissed, and paralyzed instead of using their precious time and energy to be, do, and live on purpose. This is the moment to walk your talk! If you say you want a better life, do something about it.

Are you focusing more on *looking* the part instead of *being* the part? Are your dreams dying inside on the path to pursuing the world's definition of success? It doesn't matter if you have met all of your goals, earned the degree, bought the house, or married your high school sweetheart or not. It doesn't matter if you still live with your parents, can't find a job, or can barely afford to pay your bills. It doesn't matter if you make six and seven figures a year, drive a nice car, or live in your dream home. *None of it matters* because none of it truly defines the greatness within you. None of it determines the level of joy and meaningfulness you are capable of experiencing. And absolutely none of it can you take to the grave.

> *"Comparison is the thief of joy."* — *Theodore Roosevelt*

Please don't compare yourself to anyone else. The only person you should compete with is the person you were yesterday. When you feel a competitive or comparative spirit rising up in you, go straight to the mirror and look at your *real* competition. God doesn't care whether you are broke or a billionaire. He is not moved by how much money you make. He is not excited about how well your home is decorated. He doesn't care whether you drive a Mercedes-Benz or ride a bike. We are HERE to make a difference in the lives of others. We are here to live out our destiny. It's not the quantity of our dollars; it's the depth in the *dash* in which we live that truly matters.

I invite you to start a new journey today. I invite you to shift from focusing on being successful to *being significant!* I invite you to stop settling for jobs that don't bring you joy. I invite you to stop hiding your magnificence. I invite you to wake up excited about your purpose. I invite you to use all of your gifts and operate in your greatness. I invite you to live up to your full fabulous potential. I invite you to *be ALL that you are destined to be.* THIS is your invitation to waste NO more time waiting, wishing and hoping. I invite you to rise, shine, be great and UNLEASH your unique significance!

I MATTER
I AM
SIGNIFICANT

How are you allowing life to happen instead of creating it?

_____
_____
_____
_____

In what ways are you choosing to self-abuse and play the victim role?

_____
_____
_____
_____

Who have been some of your teachers and what have you learned?

_____
_____
_____
_____

What lessons are you repeating that you do not want to repeat?

_____
_____
_____
_____

How do you truly feel about yourself?

_____

_____

_____

_____

What do you believe to be true about yourself?

_____

_____

_____

_____

Who do you need to forgive?

_____

_____

_____

_____

In what areas of your life do you need to take full responsibility and stop blaming others?

_____

_____

_____

_____

What kind of conditioning have you experienced that you want to unlearn?

_____

_____

_____

_____

What do you think your spiritual gifts are?

_____

_____

_____

_____

What would you like to see in the panoramic view of your life?

_____

_____

_____

_____

What will you focus on from this point on?

_____

_____

_____

_____

"Intuition is seeing with the soul."

— Dean Koontz

CHAPTER 2

Chapter 2
Searching for Your Significance

ACTIVATE DISCERNMENT

"What would you do if you weren't afraid? When you finally give wings to that answer then you have found your life's purpose." — *Shannon L. Alder*

Does it make you leap out of bed in the morning? Does it bring you complete soul satisfaction? Does it call your name every day? Does it make you feel wonderfully full? Does it excite you and bring an unrehearsed smile to your face? Does it make you feel bubbly and alive inside? Does it fulfill you and bring you great joy? What is "it" that I'm talking about? Your life! Unless you've decided to settle, struggle and live a mediocre life, that's what living a life of significance *will* feel like. Of course you won't experience all of this goodness *every* moment or every day, but this should be a constant and consistent feeling when you've unleashed your significance and are living out your unique purpose in life.

WHAT DO YOU WANT TO DO EVERYDAY FOR THE REST OF YOUR LIFE?

Who do you want to BE until you take your last breath? Those are two of the ultimate questions of life. And many people search for the answers for a lifetime and never seem to find them. One of the reasons people do not find these answers is because they are expecting them to show up like they imagined they would. I know this from experience. At a dark and dreadful moment in 2012, I felt like quitting and giving up on my business. From

2008-2012 I had exhausted just about every idea to become a "successful" business owner (aka = making lots of money with recognition). Imagine the white towel of surrender being aggressively thrown into the air. I was done. I was tired. That day I was determined to set myself free and end the suffering of chasing success.

I cried. That was it. I decided to quit. To wash away my tears, I decided to take a shower and just let all of the pain be washed away. Even though the surrender towel had been tossed, I still had a sliver of hope and desire to figure it out. I prayed and asked God to give me just ONE word to keep the dream alive and vowed if I heard the *one word* I would obey and fight another day. After moments of praying and crying, I clearly heard the word *"branding"* drop into my spirit like a ship's anchor into the sea. It was deep and profound.

Undeniably God gave me the word branding. I'll admit, I paused for a second in slight disbelief. After all, I was expecting a *divine* word like faith, belief or trust. I said, *"I hear you God"* and immediately jumped out without completing my shower. I ran back into the living room literally naked, and typed in my computer *"everything you need to know about branding."* When I ran back into my living room, I figuratively also grabbed that *white surrender towel* just before it hit the ground and said *"thank you God!"* Can you picture that!

The clear, undeniable, all-knowing answer was right in my face, and I doubted it, even if it were for just a second. God gave me an answer in the way I could hear and receive it, not in the way I expected it to arrive. Had the word been faith or belief I more than likely would have just shrugged it off as "my" own voice speaking instead of God's voice. God knew this. He knew I desperately needed a word I could relate to and that would be unexpected. We're always receiving the answers if we are paying attention and willing to receive them in unexpected ways. It's hard sometimes, I admit it. I, too, struggle with quieting the external nagging noise to hear the internal voice of God. I too get frustrated when the answers to my questions and prayers don't hit me like a brick. I, too, let *free will* take over sometimes and end up taking a destiny detour because I've become impatient waiting on the answer.

If you think achieving success takes too long or is hard, the search for significance can sometimes feel elusive and impossible. We have not been trained, encouraged, or conditioned to be significant. Our parents were not adequately taught how to teach us to *unleash our significance* in the world. Many of our parents were consumed with their own personal challenges, along with doing the best they could with the best they knew and had. Much of what they knew stemmed from their generational beliefs, culture, environment, socio-economic status, and, let's be real, their mental/emotional health status. I've met and counseled so many wounded children in my fifteen years of practicing therapy. Nine times out of ten when a child ended up in my counseling office, it had something to do with what parents did or did not do to or for them.

If someone grows up in a home that lacks education, is limited on problem solving skills, suffers from old wounds of abuse and or drug and alcohol addiction, how can we expect those parents to teach their children to be significant when they may feel small and unworthy themselves? If parents are struggling day to day to make ends meet, working long hours and dealing with their own mental health issues, how can we expect them to unleash the greatness within their children? Now don't get me wrong; I know there ARE parents who grew up and or raised their children in the circumstances described above and did a fantastic job. And their children rose above the circumstances to be great and do great things in the world. There are many rags to riches stories that prove this; however, those are often anomalies.

So what is significance and what does it look like to be significant in the world? Let's start with the dictionary definition. Significance is defined as *"sufficiently great, important, noteworthy, large enough to be noticed and to have an effect, and having a particular meaning.*

We could dissect this definition into a thousand pieces, but let's start with the obvious. To be significant means to matter and be great, important, remarkable, visible, impactful and meaningful. So many children grow up without hearing phrases like, *"you matter, go out into the world and be great, you are valuable to the world, be a history maker, don't dull your shine, make a difference in the world and don't worry so much about money, just do what you love and be meaningful."* Be honest; did your parent(s) say things like this to you? If they did, you are wonderfully blessed!

If you didn't hear those remarks, and still found your way to being significant, I applaud you. If you didn't hear those words and are still searching for your significance, I believe you will not only find it but unleash it; keep reading! My mother didn't necessarily say those words to me, but *she did not silence my voice*, ask me to turn down the volume on my shine, nor did she have overbearing expectations for me to accomplish certain goals. As long as I did my best and got at least C's for grades in school, she was satisfied. She didn't criticize me for being "overweight," and she didn't shame me for how I looked. I am grateful to her for that and her. You see, I could blame her for my lack of whatever, but I know my mother did the best she could with what she knew and had.

I could dwell on the fact that she didn't directly encourage me to be great and be significant in the world, or I can celebrate that she didn't break my spirit and allowed me to be me. Did your parent(s) allow you to be you? Are you allowing your children to be who they are? Do you have high expectations for you to BE successful instead of significant? I know this to be true; **you will only rise to the level of your belief**. Whatever you believe about yourself you will have, do, experience and become. Let me say it again; YOU WILL ONLY RISE TO THE LEVEL OF YOUR BELIEF. Did it sink in this time? What do you believe about you? Do you believe you are a victim or a hero? Do you believe you are average or extraordinary? Do you believe you deserve it all or just enough? Marinate on that. You will become what you believe!

"You matter, go out and be great, you are valuable to the world, be a history maker, don't dull your shine, make a difference in the world and don't worry so much about money—just do what you love and be meaningful." —- **THIS is what BEING significant is all about!**

Is YOUR life significant to the extent it makes you leap out of bed in the morning, does it bring you complete soul satisfaction, does your purpose call your name every day, do you feel wonderfully full, does your life excite you and make you smile, do you feel alive inside and does your life fulfill you and bring you great joy? If the answer is no to more than one of these questions, there could be several reasons. Let's start with purpose and does it call your name every day? If you don't know *who you are* beyond titles, degrees, fame, recognition, money, positions, affiliations, race, gender, age, religion, or physical features, there is where you begin. Some may argue against me, yet I believe who you are is far more valuable than what you have, where you live or what you look like.

You exist; therefore, you are. So who are you? I AM. Those are two of the most powerful words used together to define your existence, and the words you choose to place after I AM is who you really are. The words you choose to place after I AM is what you believe about yourself. The words you choose to place after I AM is who you will become. What are your words? What do you believe? Who are you? Go ahead; give it a try. I don't want you to choose words that describe who you *were* or words that other people have used to describe you, but instead, choose words that are true to your existence right now in this moment. Here's what my I AM looks like.

> I AM a CONSCIOUS, COMPASSIONATE, soul who feels like I have been here before. I have the gift of sensing, feeling, and knowing. Somehow I just know things. I AM WISE. I AM a true lover of people. I've spent all of my life inspiring, empowering and serving people in some way. I AM a SERVANT. I listen to my heart and follow the truth in my soul. I AM INTUITIVE. Ideas excite me, and they vividly come easy. I AM CREATIVE. Sometimes it's hard for me to rest, be still and enjoy the present moment. My mind is in a constant state of futuristic thought. I AM a VISIONARY. And because my mind is often in tomorrow, I can be a worrier. I AM IMPATIENT. I've always resented the boxes society has created for people. And for as long as I can remember, I intentionally defied the box. I despise it. I refuse to enter the box, and I love shattering the status quo. I AM a REBEL. It pains me to see suffering, abuse, and injustice inflicted upon people. It literally makes my soul ache. My heart hurts for people. My eyes weep when others are wounded and taken advantage of. I AM a

HUMANITARIAN. So of course, I must say something about it. I am not afraid to speak on topics that are taboo or unpopular. I speak with passion, zeal, conviction, transparency and often unapologetic truth. I AM a VOICE. There's so many elements, shades, levels, and variance in who I AM. I AM a BELIEVER, LOVER, WANDERER, SEEKER, HEALER, GIVER, TEACHER, and LEADER. I AM all of this and more. I AM infinite. None of them cost a dime. None of them require formal education, yet they all require a huge investment in saying yes to BEING me. This is who I AM.

You don't need anyone else's approval to BE whomever you choose to be. You don't need to ask for permission to BE who you want to be. All you have to do is choose to be, define who you want to be, and do it. Unapologetically. Boldly. Purposely. Consistently! Is it that easy? Yes it is. Pastor T.D. Jakes says, "*You got to stop waking up waiting to see what's going to happen and stop allowing other people to control what's going to happen.*" What he's saying is stop allowing life to just happen to you. Stop allowing the thoughts, words, opinions and behaviors of others to control you and your destiny. When you do this, you give away your personal power to purposely create how you experience each moment and dilute the quality of your life. And essentially, when you relinquish your personal power to CREATE YOUR OWN DESTINY, you are choosing to "self-abuse" by becoming a victim of your own choices.

Ahhhh! Now that's a truth pill that may be hard for you to swallow. Let me make it digestible for you. How much wasted energy are you giving to blaming other people for your circumstances? Are you still looking at your life and blaming your parents, past lovers, or friends and saying "*if they had not done this or that to me, my life would be different*?" Let me tell you something about this destiny killer. While you are sitting around blaming them for the current status of your life, they have moved on and are enjoying life. They are not thinking about you or what they've done to you. They have left you holding a big bag of bondage, and, either you can drop that bag and let it go, or you can keep clinging to it and continue to be captive in your own choices.

Let's get back to the "IT" I spoke of in the beginning of the chapter. I asked you if your IT makes you leap out of bed, bring your complete soul satisfaction, call your name, make you feel wonderfully full, excite you, make you smile, give you great joy or make you feel bubbly and alive inside. Again, when I speak of IT, I'm referring to your significance and your purpose. Your significance is not tied to what other people think of you or what they say about you. It's intimately intertwined in WHAT you say about yourself and WHO you believe you are.

Purpose. *What is it? How do you find it? What if you've been searching for it and can't seem to find it?* The answers to these questions are infinite and complex, but let me attempt to give you some answers that finally make sense for you. I was delighted to find clarity in these answers while reading a passage by Doris Lessing, where she talks about how we are briefed on our purpose shortly before birth. She says this...

"God gives us the brief before our birth, before our soul's descent into flesh. But after our births we remember the briefing only dimly, because taking on a body weakens the ability of the spirit to remember who we are and what we're here for. – So the nagging sense of having forgotten something important, the longing without cause, the calls that haunt us like whispers from a little too far away, come from our remembering parts and fragments of the briefing. The calling is not forgotten entirely, but is muted and fuzzy, like a distant radio station whose signal is filled with static."

Oh how true this is! – Your purpose is NOT a mystery. It's not a figment of your imagination. It's not this made up thing that you'll never find, and it's not only for "special" people. Every person has a purpose, or they would not be here. Either you can reconnect with spirit and get back in alignment with your pre-determined purpose or you can continue to exercise your own free will and do it your way. Many times when you do it your way, you never find the path to your purpose.

Let's consider the possibility that what Doris Lessing says is true (and I believe it is); the first key to discovering your purpose is to *remember* who you are. She talked about the body weakening the ability of the spirit to remember. That means the spirit, your creator, *has the answer*. Thus the further away from spirit (God), and the more we are in our body (consumed with the natural state of our being), the less we remember about our purpose, our unique assignment in the world, our significance.

If you are still searching for your purpose, start by reconnecting to your source, your spirit, and your creator. Your purpose is already within you; you just have to remember it. You remember by canceling out any and all definitions, labels and titles you've allowed the world (and you) to put on you. You remember by re-defining who you really are and declaring your bodacious I AM. You remember who you are by choosing to not allow others to victimize you and that includes yourself. You remember by decreasing the static of the outside world and tuning into the frequency of who you desire to be and who your creator says you are. You remember by intentionally listening to the whispers of your soul and nudges of your intuition. All of the answers you seek are there. Make the choice today to go inward to get and receive them.

As you continue on your inward search for the answers to the question *"what am I here to do,"* they will also be revealed to you. Everyone at some point in their life struggles with uncovering the answers to this universal question. If you don't know what you're here to do or need clarity on what you're here to do, don't worry; it will become clear as you read on. I used to complicate the process of discovering my purpose, and honestly, at times, there are parts of the path to my destiny that become frustrating and fuzzy. They become fuzzy when I move too far away from God and think that I can walk out my destiny alone. They become fuzzy when I lead with my EGO (Edging God Out) and or exercise free will without consultation with my creator. We are not meant to live this life alone or to full our destiny by ourselves. A destiny fulfilled is co-created between you and your creator.

"Our prime purpose in this life is to help others. And if you can't help them, at least don't hurt them." – Dalai Lama

Don't overcomplicate the purpose of your *purpose*. We are here to do two main things; *to love and to serve others.* I believe there are two primary emotions (feelings) all human beings experience: *love and fear.* We either experience love or versions of it, or we experience fear and the various forms of it. Think of these emotional experiences as a continuum if you will.

LOVE ——————————— NEUTRAL ——————————— FEAR

Within this continuum we experience love feelings, such as joy, pleasure, happiness, excitement, gratitude, peace and or appreciation. Also within this continuum, we experience fear feelings, such as hate, despair, anger, sadness, doubt and or jealousy. Simply put LOVE feelings feel good, and FEAR feelings don't. At any given moment, you can quickly identify whether you are in a loving or fearful state. This is powerful because it serves as a cue for you to *choose* how you want to feel in every moment. It's not always easy, but it is *your* choice.

So how will you first begin loving yourself? When you doubt, worry, complain, compare, and blame, *you are choosing to be in a state of fear, thus abusing yourself.* You are the perpetrator of your own victimization. Let that statement REALLY sink in. You begin to love yourself by believing you are enough just as you are. You begin to love yourself by accepting what is and working to make it what you want it to be. Resisting or denying what is… creates unnecessary self-inflicted suffering. Accepting what is… ushers in truth and creates peace. Choosing personal acceptance creates peace, and *being at peace with you is an act of love.* This is where you begin. You ARE enough. Accept where you are right now and choose to be and do better.

This same philosophy applies to how you love others. Are you expressing doubt and disbelief in others? Are you spending too much time complaining about what they do or don't do? Are you comparing them to someone else or an ideal person? Are you blaming others for your feelings, choices and circumstances? If you're honest with yourself, the answer may be yes to all of the above. Why? Because often, I find myself doing the same things, and then I remember acting in love or fear is a choice. Sometimes I can let go and move on quickly, and other times it takes a while. Eventually, I know I must stop the FEAR behavior, so I can be free and be in a space of love.

Your purpose is to love yourself, love others, love your gifts, love what you do and love serving others with your gifts. Yes! **Your purpose is not complicated!** What if it is this simple? I believe it is. Are you ready to remember or recharge your purpose and be significant in the world? *Who do you want to BE until you take your last breath*? This is where your journey to unleashing your significance begins… Lace up your destiny shoes; let's go on this journey together.

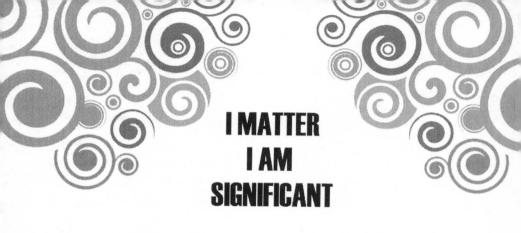

I MATTER
I AM
SIGNIFICANT

In what ways are you settling, struggling and living in mediocrity?

_____

_____

_____

_____

Who do you want to be until you take your last breath?

_____

_____

_____

_____

In what ways have you heard God's voice but dismissed it or didn't believe it?

_____

_____

_____

_____

How would you like God to speak to you so you can take action?

_____

_____

_____

_____

What did you learn from your parent(s) and upbringing that you want to unlearn or break the cycle?

_____

_____

_____

_____

In what ways are you still living in the past?

_____

_____

_____

_____

How do you define success?

_____

_____

_____

_____

How do you define significance?

_____

_____

_____

_____

Are you average or extraordinary? Why?

_____

_____

_____

_____

In what ways are you seeking approval from others or waiting on permission?

_____
_____
_____
_____

Who are you blaming and what are you blaming them for?

_____
_____
_____
_____

What is your purpose in the world?

_____
_____
_____
_____

What hunches, nudges or whispers have you experienced that are leading you to your purpose?

_____
_____
_____
_____

What are some of your ego's favorite ways to sabotage you?

_____
_____
_____
_____

Are you living a more fear driven life or love driven life and how?

_____

_____

_____

_____

What do you love about you?

_____

_____

_____

_____

In what ways do you best serve the world?

_____

_____

_____

_____

"What we fear most is usually what we most need to do."

– Tim Ferriss

CHAPTER 3

Chapter 3

Creating the Capacity for Your Calling

ACTIVATE COURAGE

"In the process of letting go you will lose many things from the past, but you will find yourself." – Deepak Chopra

Are you ready? Let's go! We've got fears to conquer, doubts to destroy and dreams to fulfill! One thing I know for sure is, you cannot pick up your purpose if your hands are filled with joy-stealing junk! It's time for you to let go, drop the baggage, dump the junk and create the capacity to carry your calling. Do you have a space in your home, such as a drawer or a closet that is filled with anything and everything? A space where every time you search for something you need or something important you can't find it because it's full of junk and unnecessary stuff? You vow to clean it out one day, yet stuff keeps piling up and cluttering the space. Finally, you say enough is enough, and you purge the space by throwing out everything that has no use, serves no purpose, is old and raggedy, and stuff that no longer has meaning or value in your life. You may even hold on to some stuff for a little while longer just in case you need it, but chances are you never will.

That's exactly what I want you to do with your soul container. Your heart. Your mind. Your spirit. *Let that crap go!* Release it, set yourself free, and empty your hands so you can pick up your purpose, fulfill your destiny and unleash your significance. And don't hold on to something (or someone) you think you're going to need knowing damn well you don't. Drop it! Don't be afraid; you can do this. You got this. And, if you are afraid do it anyway. You're going to be surprised to find out that most of what you refuse to let go of is your OWN junk. Yeah, you'll soon see that it's not *them* holding you back; it's you. Much of your suffering is self-inflicted.

> *"Suffering is not holding you. You are holding suffering. When you become good at the art of letting sufferings go, then you'll come to realize how unnecessary it was for you to drag those burdens around with you. You'll see that no one else other than you was responsible. The truth is that existence wants your life to become a festival."* —Osho

Fear are the lies we tell ourselves to avoid telling the truth, taking responsibility, owning our stuff, speaking our truth, shining our light, loving ourselves and others and doing our work. I remember the fear I carried for forty years about what would happen when I discovered the truth about who my father was or was not. It took me forty years to finally be courageous enough to seek the truth. Over that forty-year span, I also carried some shame, resentment, anger, and sadness. While it may seem justified that because I didn't know who my biological father was, I somehow deserved the right to carry those fear feelings. In retrospect, the only right I was entitled to was the right to live by chance and circumstance or live by choice. I chose all three. I chose to avoid not knowing the truth, I *chose* to be a victim of my circumstances (to self-abuse), and eventually, I chose to brave my way to learning the truth.

In 2011, I finally found the courage to make contact with the man who my mother told me was my father. I called him and said I am ready to know the truth. He, too, wanted to know the truth, and so we set up an appointment to have a DNA test done. Three weeks prior to the test we had several phone conversations and got to know each other better. We both agreed that no matter what the results were that we would still stay connected. We met in a city outside of my home town, Sioux City, Iowa about thirty minutes away and took an easy oral swab test. Three weeks later, I received the results in the mail that read ZERO percent chance we had any matching DNA. I must admit, I was disappointed and a little sad. He was such a nice man, and we had begun to build a friendship. I called him with the results, and, to my surprise, he expressed feeling disappointed and sad, too.

I did it! I faced a fear to discover a bittersweet truth. Bitter because he was not my father, and I had carried emotional baggage (known and unknown) in my body and spirit for 40 years. For at least the first 20 years, that baggage was bitterness, resentment and sadness; towards a man who didn't deserve it. This moment was sweet; however, because in those conversations prior to the results, I spoke with and to him from a place of forgiveness, love, understanding, compassion and peace. I didn't have one negative feeling through the whole process. It was sweet because he said these words to me.

"I wish you were my daughter; you are a phenomenal woman. I am so proud of you for your accomplishments and the woman you have become. Whoever your father is, he is a blessed man and doesn't even know it." He then offered to be a surrogate father, a father figure if ever I needed one, and I accepted his beautiful gift without hesitation. We still keep in touch today, and I AM grateful for him.

Wow, see what happens when you dare to face your fears! Things can turn out better than the nightmare you imagine in your mind. The most fascinating part of this experience is that we both are FREE! We know the truth, and, because we said "yes" to tell the truth, the chains of bondage were broken. When we both take our last breath, we will *know* the truth. We won't carry any "what ifs" to the grave. I don't know about you, but I want to die empty. By empty, I mean *free* from hurt, anger, pain and resentment. By free, I mean having used up my gifts until they are dried out and having poured out so much love for others there is none left. By free, I mean having taking all the risks I possibly could have and by daring enough to live my dreams. By free, I mean having unleashed every powerful, brilliant, magnificent and glorious part of who I AM into the world. I dare you to face your fears and see what's on the other side. No matter what it is, you will survive and rise up stronger!

For at least twenty years, I chose to self-abuse by harboring toxic feelings and blaming someone else for my pain. Thank God for "old soul" wisdom (as if I have been here before) because it allowed me at a young age to take responsibility for how I wanted to feel and to take responsibility for creating my destiny on my own terms. What negative feelings are you harboring that are essentially killing your spirit? What purpose are they serving? What have you got to lose or gain by releasing them? You can choose to stay a prisoner of your own pain or you can set yourself free; you are the *only* key holder.

THIS is worth repeating. It's not *them* holding you back; it's you. Much of your suffering is self-inflicted. You will not carry out your purpose, complete your divine assignment, or fulfill your destiny when your soul container is full of fear, resentment, blame and bitterness. You cannot carry out your purpose if you don't have the capacity to contain it. Are you ready to purge yourself to unleash the possibilities of your unlimited potential? Let's start by taking the lid off of your greatness! There's one word that unequivocally serves as the great lever to lifting your lid and that word is *truth*.

Before we begin to manipulate the great lever, let's talk about *the* lid. Of course we know the primary function of a lid is to cover something up, to keep things in, to keep something from being exposed and more. However, I want to introduce or re-introduce you to another perspective and theory about "the lid." New York Times Best-Selling Author, Speaker and Leadership Expert, John C. Maxwell is widely known for his theory, which includes a book and lecture series on *The 21 Irrefutable Laws of Leadership*. Let me take a step back. Remember I said you are here to love and serve; that is the ultimate purpose for all of humanity. Don't get this thing twisted. *Your life is not only for you*. You are here to be of service to others and to lead. Yes, you are a leader! That may not mean that you lead like Dr. Martin Luther King, Oprah Winfrey, the CEO of a company, or the President of the United States. What it means is there is a group of people *you* were created to lead, a cause you are meant to lead or a movement you are meant to lead.

Maybe the group of people are your family. Maybe the group of people are in your church. Maybe the group of people are at work, a team, or in your community. And maybe your leadership assignment is to be the leader in your *own* life. Don't shy away from being a leader because you *are* here to lead someone or something. The first law John C. Maxwell talks about in his book, *The 21 Irrefutable Laws of Leadership* is *The Law of the Lid,* which states, "leadership ability is the lid that determines a person's level of effectiveness.

The lower an individual's ability to lead, the lower the lid on his/her potential. The higher the individual's ability to lead, the higher the lid on his potential."–What does this have to do with you and your lid? If you want to make an impact in the world, you need to be able to influence people, and your ability to influence people greatly depends on your ability to lead.

Change whether big or small is always orchestrated and instigated by leaders. Without leaders, things and situations stay the same. Let's keep it simple. If you want to see and experience change in your life, you must step up and become the leader of your own life. Your purpose won't necessarily chase you down, and destiny will not always knock on your door. You must *choose* to lead your life in the direction of purpose and destiny. Even if you are here to transform the lives within your family, you must *say yes* to greater leadership and it starts by lifting your lid. So what does lifting your lid really look like? Reflect on your life as it is right now. Are you living in the past? Are you stagnant and stuck in place? Do things seem to not be improving or moving forward? If you are living in the past, stuck, or not progressing, your lid is tight, and you are NOT leading your life in the direction you desire it to go.

The first step in lifting your lid is recognizing the need to raise it. The second step is to tell the *truth* (the great lever) about why your lid is tight. The third step is assessing your performance as a leader. Do you have clear goals and are you working towards exceeding them daily? Have you identified your strengths and are you maximizing them in every moment? Are you willing to claim your limitations and ask for help from those who have what you need? Do you have a clear vision and do you know what your final destination is? It's time to tell the truth (the great lever). Maybe you are showing up in your own life as a stand in or a stage hand, instead of owning your power and playing the leading role. If you're taking what you get and or letting life just happen to you, you are *not* leading your life; you are *allowing* life to drag you.

Let's take a closer look at your lid. The reason your lid may be tight and or your leadership performance is lacking is because your lid is weighted down with emotional clutter and junk. Boy do I know all about this truth! I can recall several moments in my life when the bricks of life were stacked on top of my personal life lid. One moment in particular was between the years of 2011-2012 (during the same time, I threw in the white surrender towel). I had a lot going on in my life.

My business wasn't thriving at the rate I wanted and needed it to. My son went off to college and returned home after deciding it was not right for him. I was frustrated in my business. And, I had moved away from my family for the first time to Dallas, Texas. Whew! I was well outside of my comfort zone. In fact, it felt like I was in the *Twilight Zone* for real. Nothing was familiar. Not much was working. I felt like I was in a strange land. I was overwhelmed. My intention was to move to Dallas for a fresh start, secure a place to call home, and bring my son to Texas with me. I had *never* left him. Parents aren't supposed to leave their children; well, that's my belief at least; plus, he wasn't quite ready to leave Omaha.

So I moved to Dallas with my husband in October 2011. Within two weeks, we moved into an apartment, and I immediately told my son, we got a new home, and I want you come here and be with us. He assured me he was coming. Week after week he assured me he was coming, and I insisted on going to get him. He said he would come for Christmas. Christmas passed. More weeks went by, and he finally said, "*Mom, I don't want to move to Dallas.*" He was nineteen. He was still my baby. He was not grown in my eyes, and I felt he still needed his parent's guidance. Finally, I accepted that he did not want to leave Omaha. So, he stayed with my mother. That gave me some peace of mind, but my spirit was never ever settled.

I tried to make the most of my time in Dallas, but a big part of my heart was in Omaha with my only child. I visited Omaha 2-3 times within that year, and, on the final visit in December of 2012, I decided to stay. I called my husband and told him, and he understood because he watched me emotionally struggle with being away from my son while in Dallas. We agreed it was time to come back to what we knew as home. I had so many life bricks on my lid there were times I felt like I couldn't breathe. I felt a bit suffocated by life. I knew I had to do something, and moving back to Omaha removed half of those bricks. I was able to catch my breath and take back my power to become the leader of my life.

What's on top of your lid right now? Are you dealing with family drama? Are you going through a divorce? Have you lost someone you loved dearly? Are you in a relationship that's toxic? Are you overwhelmed with caring for elderly parents? Do you not have enough money coming in? Or are you dealing with a multitude of various personal challenges? Whatever life bricks are sitting on your lid you can either let the weight of them suffocate your life or you can choose today to ditch the bricks! You might already know it's time to ditch the bricks but may not know exactly how to do it. There is no secret or mysterious formula. You just have to reach a point where you are sick and tired of being sick and tired and do something about it.

You don't DECIDE to do something, you CHOOSE to do something, and you take immediate, repeated, and consistent action until you receive your desired result. That's it. That is the way you change your circumstances. Deciding is a psychological state of contemplation. It means you are seriously considering doing something. Choosing is a physical state of *being*. It means you *will* take action. For example, when you say "*I'm deciding which book to buy,*" you have not taken action yet; however, when you say "*I'm choosing this book,*" you have acted upon your decision. Taking too much time thinking about what you *should* do to remove the life bricks from your lid won't remove them.

> *"Taking action is hard, but you know what? Enduring a bad situation can be its own hell." – Whoopi Goldberg*

You start by identifying the bricks! These are people, places, events, spaces, ideals, rules, expectations, opinions, thoughts and or behaviors that illicit FEAR feelings. Who or what in your life sets off feelings of pain, doubt, worry, frustration, anger, or shame in your life? What in your life feels burdensome? What or who in your life feels like they are blocking the path to your purpose, potential or destiny? Remember the importance of *truth*, the great lever as you identify the bricks. Some of the people adding weight to your life may be people you love, such as family and friends. The truth can hurt, and once the pain subsides, it sets you free.

At last, we must specifically address this "self-abuse" I keep talking about. I have legitimately been hurt by too many people to count, but I've hurt myself even more than that by choosing to exaggerate the experience. *Don't act like you don't know what I'm talking about.* We have the tendency to drag things out longer than they should be and create long suffering in our lives. Hey, don't get me wrong, I understand it takes time to heal and rebound from pain. I'm certainly not discounting your experience, and we're all different. Some of us can bounce back faster than others. However, you know you've dragged out drama at least one time in your life; admit it.

In every second of our lives we can choose to be victims of our circumstances or heroes of our destiny. Did you know that the "victim-stance" is actually a thinking error? Thinking errors are defined as *irrational thinking patterns that cause you to feel bad and self-sabotage.*

We all have thinking errors, but you can learn how to identify and rectify them so they do not ruin your life. An example of a common thinking error is *Black and White Thinking.* This type of thought pattern causes you to think in terms of right or wrong and good and bad. Black and White Thinking prevents you from seeing the grey moments and actually causes you to be less empathetic towards others. Another example of a thinking error would be *Mindreading.* When you frequently try to imagine what other people are thinking, or you become obsessed with believing you *know* what other people are thinking, you end up creating unnecessary chaos and suffering. This leads to false assumptions, and you begin to exaggerate, stretch the truth, and or make things up where there is no evidence to do so.

Others thinking errors *include labeling, filtering, justifying, blaming, personalizing, over generalizing, and denial,* to name a few. If you just consider the possibility that you have *Black and White Thinking* and *Mindreading* as thinking errors, can you see how much potential self-inflicted pain you can create for yourself? Your thoughts dictate the way you feel and behave so to change your circumstances you must start with how you think. Take a look at the partial list of behaviors below and see if you can determine the possible thoughts that would produce these types of behaviors. And, while you're reviewing the list, be honest about how many times in a day, month or year you behave like this.

VICTIM-STANCE THOUGHTS & BEHAVIORS

- You feel burdened more than you feel blessed.
- When things go wrong, you often blame others instead of acknowledging your contribution to the chaos in your life.
- You often think, feel, or say *"why me?"*
- You're frequently irritated, annoyed, and frustrated by life challenges.
- You spend a lot of time nit-picking and complaining about small things.
- When you see other people succeeding, you secretly wonder how they did it, wish you were them, or have a hard time being truly happy for them.
- You have the tendency to make mountains out of small things and often get stuck in the worst case scenario.

TAKE A CLOSER LOOK AT VICTIM STANCE BEHAVIOR AND THE POSSIBLE THINKING ERRORS THAT CAUSE THE BEHAVIORS

VICTIM-STANCE BEHAVIOR	THINKING ERROR THAT CAUSES THE BEHAVIOR
You feel burdened more than you feel blessed.	**FILTERING:** Filtering out the positives in your life causes you to only see the negative and creates a doom and gloom mindset.

When things go wrong you often blame others instead of acknowledging your contribution to the chaos in your life.	**BLAMING:** Blaming others and failing to take responsibility leads to personal captivity and false projection on others.
You often think, feel, or say "why me?"	**CONTROL ERROR**: Seeing yourself as a helpless victim and being controlled externally prevents you from taking responsibility and moving forward.
You're frequently irritated, annoyed, and frustrated by life challenges.	**BLACK & WHITE THINKING**: When you see situations or things as either or grey moments make you upset because your thought pattern is inflexible.
You spend a lot of time nit-picking and complaining about small things.	**BEING RIGHT:** You think your way is the best and only way and anything outside of that must be wrong.
When you see other people succeeding you secretly wonder how they did it, wish you were them, or have a hard time being truly happy for them.	**UNREAL IDEAL:** Comparing yourself to others inhibits your ability to acknowledge their greatness and honor your own.
You have the tendency to make mountains out of small things and often get stuck in the worst case scenario.	**CATASTROPHISING:** Thinking the worst is going to happen when there is no logical evidence, causes you to magnify situations and become overly stressed.

Can you see the power of your thoughts? Can you see how your thoughts evoke your feelings and your feelings dictate your behavior? Can you see how your behavior will either sabotage or support your purpose? No one is in control of your thoughts but you. If you don't like your circumstances, choose to think differently. It's not impossible! You can do this. *Are you ready to release your history in order to step into your destiny?*

Here are a few strategies to help you take off the bricks, lift your lid and lighten your load. Today is the day that you *choose* to let go of your own stuff and take responsibility for the direction of your life. Today is the day you stop the self-inflicted suffering. You can do it!

#1 — You may not know exactly what you WANT, but I bet you know WHAT YOU DON'T WANT. Take out a sheet of paper, and, on the front, write the heading *"what I don't want"* and on the back write *"what I do want"* and start making your list. I've found that when you start acknowledging what you don't want you soon discover what you really do want. Intentionally, mindfully, courageously and consistently move away from and eliminate what you don't want, in your life every day. As you start to eliminate what you don't want, you get clarity about what you do want, and you begin creating the capacity to contain your calling. I'll share more about this in a later chapter.

#2 — Think about your thoughts every day. Yes, it is possible and oh so necessary. Learn to pause when you think. Learn to rewind when you think. Stop right now. What are you thinking about? Why are you thinking it? What is the message in your thoughts? Where did the thoughts come from? How are your thoughts creating your current experience? Do you like how you feel right now? Does it feel like fear, or does it feel like love? Is there truth in your thoughts? Do they make sense? What will happen in your life within the next thirty minutes if you continue to think the thoughts you are thinking? – Whew! Are you tired or confused yet? Don't be. This is powerful, and it will help change your circumstances. You must become a master at *Metacognition*, thinking about your thinking or cognition about cognition. This isn't strange or odd behavior; you've done it before, but just didn't know you were doing it. Have you ever rehearsed what you will say during an interview or when you have to tell someone bad news? Yes? If so, you were practicing *Metacognition*. When you think about your thinking, it causes you to be mindful, intentional, and deliberate, and gives you the opportunity to check in to see if your thoughts are being distorted by a mental filter, such as the ones in the graph a few pages back. Reckless thinking, mental filters, and unchecked thoughts lead to soul container chaos and bricks on your lid.

#3 — Pleasure can lead you to your purpose and moments of delight will illuminate the path of your destiny. Remember you both think and act in love or fear. So it makes perfect sense that pleasure and delight is derived from love. What is pleasurable to you? What makes you feel good? Who pushes your joy button? Who or what makes you feel alive inside? What places, events, and activities stimulate you and delight your soul? When you are unsure of what you want, pay attention to what feels pleasurable and delightful. That's your soul's way of saying *"yes more of this please!"* Many times thinking about what you want doesn't always work. Therefore, it's critical that you *feel* your way to your purpose. *Your soul knows the way.* Listen to it. Follow it with faith that your inner navigation system already knows the destination and intuitively you do too. Discover what delights you, and do more of it. Identify who brings you joy and pleasure, and spend more time with them. Go to the places that make you feel alive inside as often as you can. Your soul knows the way; listen to it.

You're here to be significant! A life of significance is created and lived from the inside out. You cannot carry what you cannot contain. You can't love if you cannot carry love for yourself. You cannot teach courage if you cannot first be courageous for you. You cannot help others become happy if happiness does not have a home within you. A colander cannot hold water. You know the kitchen tool you use to strain pasta? No matter what liquid you pour into it, it will leak out. It will never contain it. And the same is true for you; you cannot carry your calling if you don't have the capacity to contain it. It's time to patch up the holes in your soul container.

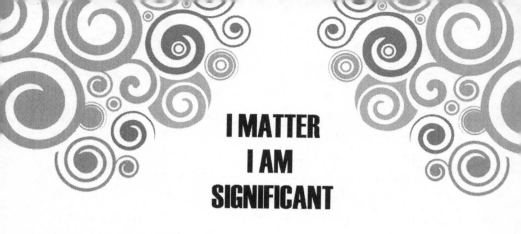

I MATTER
I AM
SIGNIFICANT

In what ways is your life cluttered?

_____
_____
_____
_____

What do you need to release and let go of?

_____
_____
_____
_____

In what ways are you creating your own suffering?

_____
_____
_____
_____

What do you need to tell the truth about?

_____
_____
_____
_____

What truth do you need to know in order to move forward?

_____

_____

_____

_____

How has being afraid affected your life?

_____

_____

_____

_____

What fears do you need or want to face?

_____

_____

_____

_____

How are you holding yourself back?

_____

_____

_____

_____

What bricks are on top of your lid?

_____

_____

_____

_____

How can you step up and be the leader of your own life?

_____

_____

_____

_____

What is the vision for your life?

_____

_____

_____

_____

What have you been thinking about doing that you are now willing to do something about it?

_____

_____

_____

_____

What thinking errors (thoughts) are keeping you stuck and unfulfilled in your life?

_____

_____

_____

_____

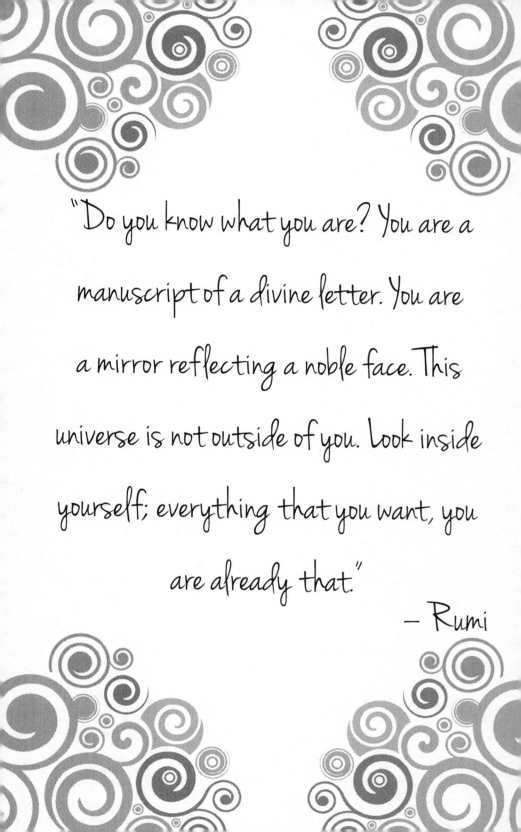

"Do you know what you are? You are a manuscript of a divine letter. You are a mirror reflecting a noble face. This universe is not outside of you. Look inside yourself; everything that you want, you are already that."

— Rumi

CHAPTER 4

Chapter 4

Your Soul Knows the Way

ACTIVATE TRUST

"Life shrinks or expands in proportion to one's courage." – Anais Nin

I believe you've been called into the land of the living to do something significant; and it's simple. *You are here to BE significant.* The path to your significance will never look like mine or anyone else's. Accepting this truth will alleviate an enormous amount of the suffering you endure. By suffering, I mean the *self-abuse* that comes with comparison, score keeping, and envying the lives that other people live. You can't have their destiny. You can't have their life. You can't have their relationships, friends and "success." None of it is meant for you!

I was guilty. Many times I found myself peeking in the windows of other people's purpose or standing outside their big glorious house wondering what they did to get this beautiful home. And then, begrudgingly, walking past their glorious show of success and wondering, *what's wrong with me that I can't have a home like that.* I questioned whether I was chasing a dream I'd never catch or was it just not *my* time. From afar, I'd swoon over the notoriety and recognition that many of my colleagues and friends were experiencing in their business and wondered when *my time* was coming. And, if I can be brutally honest, I wondered what tricks they played, lies they told or schemes they orchestrated to get all the money, fame, followers and publicity they were receiving.

That sounds crazy doesn't it? *Well, I guess you are crazy too!* Don't act like you've never looked at someone else's life and wished you had it.

Don't act like you haven't swooned over someone else's success and envied them. Don't act like you've never discounted people's genius or hustle and speculated that it was possibly a scam of some sorts. Every single time I behaved this way I discounted my own brilliance and genius. Every time I questioned someone else's greatness I minimized my own magnificence. And, every time I was envious of someone else's fruit, I forgot who I AM. I betrayed myself. I doubted my creator and turned my back on my soul's truth. I lost my way.

In those moments of covetous voyeurism, I felt disappointed, defeated, and doubtful. And, when I snapped out of the delusion of death by comparison, I felt guilty that I doubted God and myself. Sometimes the delusion lasted for moments and other times days. I was sleeping on my significance. I'm grateful to have a bounce back spirit because I know some people fall into the pit of pity and don't climb out, don't know how to climb out and or refuse to climb out. If you haven't found yourself sleeping in the delusion of comparison, you're not being honest with yourself. Every human being does it, has done it, and on some level will do it again and again in the future. Why? Because we are imperfectly human.

It's easy to believe the grass is greener on the other side especially if you have not tilled your soil, laid down high quality seeds and are too busy peeking in the window of someone else's purpose to cultivate your own grass. The next time you see someone with very green grass, instead of wondering how it's so lush and vibrant, admire it, celebrate it, and courageously ask the landscaper how they achieved the green greatness. If you're open to learning, they just might teach you a thing or two. However, I believe you already know *what* to do. You may not know exactly *how* to accomplish it, but you know because your soul already knows the way.

The knowing comes in the form of gut checks, nudges in your spirit, whispers from the Divine One and in the glimpses of delicious inspiration. Gut checks show up like flashing warning signs signaling you to be cautious, to walk away or get out. The nudges in your spirit are saying "*yes do that, go for it and take the leap.*" Whispers from the Divine One are the love language that says *"it's going to be alright, trust me, and go forward in faith."* And glimpses of delicious inspiration are direct instructions and ideas given to you by the Divine One. Did you know that inspiration essentially means *"to be in spirit?"* So when you feel inspired to do something that is the Divine One, God speaking directly to you.

Are you taking action on your inspiration? My desperate and miserable moment in the shower turned out to be an inspirational catalyst that catapulted me into the next level of my business and life. I could have dismissed it because it didn't show up like I expected it to, and, who knows, maybe had I done that, I wouldn't be sharing this message with you. When you experience inspirational moments, those are whispers from the Divine One, and when you act on them, you can create magic and meaningful experiences. *The soul knows.* It always knows the way.

Let me help you believe even more that your soul knows. I bet at least one time in your life you've experienced a Déjà vu moment. Those mysterious, magical and a bit eerie moments when you feel like you've been in a particular moment before. You're wearing the same clothes, in the same place, and doing the same thing as if you already experienced that moment in the past. Déjà vu literally means "already seen" and that's exactly how you feel when you have a Déjà vu moment. There's tons of research available about this phenomenon, and I'll leave that up to you to explore. There is one element of Déjà vu I do want to discuss as it relates to your soul knowing the way.

In a 2012 study, researchers offered a possible explanation of Déjà vu being Cryptomnesia; aka when learned information is forgotten, stored in the brain and invoked when one is in a similar situation. I won't get all scientific or metaphysical on you, but when you experience those Déjà vu moments, don't they feel strikingly REAL? Whatever the cause behind Déjà vu, you get the sense that your soul or your spirit is speaking to you and saying *"yes, you've been here before, you've done this before, and or you've experienced this before."* I don't know what the scientific or psychological cause of Déjà vu is, yet I believe that the "knowing" we experience is startling, profound and powerful. I further believe your soul has your purpose stored in your memory just the same. I don't believe *any* person is born for no reason. There is a purpose for everyone. There *is* a purpose for you.

Maybe you're still searching for your purpose. Maybe you know what it is. And, maybe you want to become clearer and convicted in your purpose and amplify it. The latter is where I am in my life. I know why I exist, who I AM, and what I'm here to accomplish. You reading this book and saying "yes" to your significance is a big part of my divine assignment. Even I need to hear the whispers of the Divine One. I too long for the glimpses of my greatness to be revealed to me. And yes, I, still today require gut checks to remind me that *I matter*, that I have greatness within me, and I AM significant in the world. I know my soul knows the way, and I'm learning how to dial into the frequency of my soul so that I can hear its undeniable message. There is more for me to be, do, experience and offer this world. I've said yes to my significance, and I hope you do too.

IMAGINE if you said a full body YES to your magnificence, your greatness, your genius and your brilliance. Just think of what YOU could be, do, have and experience. Dimming your light is a dis-service to the world. There's absolutely nothing wrong with walking in your greatness, shining your light and using your magnificence to make a meaningful difference in the world. Your soul already knows the answers to this question. What would your life be like if you said YES to your significance? Thinking about what could happen will not create the experience of it; only in your choosing will you *know* for sure.

Over the years I've gotten lots of spiritual nudges to say "yes" to my purpose and significance. Some of the nudges were subtle while others were in my face wakeup calls. The soul always knows how to get your attention especially when you've been ignoring the subtle nudges. I recall this moment I am about to share with you like it happened yesterday. I'll never forget this day. I truly believe this was God's way of saying, *"Look Catrice, I'm tired of tickling your spirit and whispering in your ear, let me give you something you can feel, let me show you how significant you really are."* The following is part of my story I shared in my third book, *The Art of Fear-Free Living*. This was one of my biggest wakeup calls. [updated excerpt]

From Money Focused to Mission Driven

Before I left my full-time job in 2008, I was making pretty good money, didn't worry about bills, had health and dental insurance and was living with little financial stress and struggle. I had read many times that before leaving your job to start a business you should save at least 6 months of income to have as start up and living funds. I originally started my business in 2005 after being laid off from work twice in a row. I knew then I had to put my financial security in my own hands. I started putting together my business plan and had a decent foundation set for my speaking, training and consulting company. There was something comforting about knowing I could be in control of my life, time, freedom and finances. However, it was more comforting at the time to rely on a steady flow of income, so after the second lay off I looked for a job and found one that paid me well.

I was now working at the full-time job that I eventually left before starting my business. I went in early, stayed late, volunteered to be on committees, took on extra projects, developed programs, served on the management team and wrote grants to bring large amounts of money into the organization. I put my heart, soul, blood, sweat and tears into developing a diversity program that not only pulled in a hefty amount of grant dollars, but brought amazing, positive attention to the program. The program was going well until I suggested that we as an organization do what we asked other organizations to do, work on strengthening our commitment to a particular cause so we could walk the walk.

It started off spectacular but turned sour very quickly when the personal expectations and challenges became too great for the staff. It was clear to me many of them only wanted to talk about it but didn't want to be about it. I went from SheRo to Shit-Starter in the blink of an eye. Deep in my soul I always knew there was something greater I was supposed to do in life. I knew with every fiber of my being that I had a gift that was sitting on the back shelf because I was afraid to step out of my financial comfort zone. I was convinced that employer after employer had no clue of the value I brought to their organization. I knew I was a pawn in a chess game set up for me to never really win. I was tired of working my butt off to raise someone else's revenue. I was tired of creating winning programs to only leave all my intellectual property behind. I was sick and tired of being sick and tired.

In the winter of 2007 I went in for a routine doctor's visit. I was anemic and had not been taking my iron pills. I knew my doctor was going to take blood samples, and she would get on me about not following her orders. After the appointment, I stopped by the local pharmacy, picked up some iron pills and went back home. Once I got home, I checked my voice mail messages and the first one I receive was from my doctor. The message went a little something like this, "Catrice, your hemoglobin is extremely low. I need you to come back in and check into the hospital." I went into a state of panic and worry and immediately went back to the hospital. I was informed my hemoglobin was 5.5 and the normal range for women was between 12 and 16. Basically, I was "walking dead." Hemoglobin carries oxygen to your organs and major organs such as your brain and heart and mine weren't getting an adequate supply.

I was presented with two options: go home and work on getting my hemoglobin up by myself or take a blood transfusion. I couldn't take the risk of failing to raise my hemoglobin, so I decided to get the blood transfusion. It was not an easy choice. My late grandmother always preached about how it was a sin to take body parts and fluids from another human being and that God didn't like that. I found myself in a spiritual dilemma and finally made the decision to go through with the transfusion. I made the choice because I wanted to *live; I wanted to be around for my son and husband. I wanted to live out my dreams.*

While lying there watching the first drop of someone else's blood go into my veins, I prayed and begged God to let this procedure be complication free. All the life changing questions went through my mind, "Am I living on purpose, am I doing God's will for my life, am I living out my purpose and dreams etc?" The answers to all of those questions was no. I prayed to God to give me another chance to live and to do what my soul was calling me to do. God answered my prayers abundantly. I experienced a "Soul Eruption" (the spawning of my first book entitled Soul Eruption, released in 2009).

I woke up from the procedure, went home and said "this is it, it's now or never." I spent most of Saturday talking to God, praising him, thanking him and asking for faith and courage. I spent most of Sunday drafting my resignation letter and experienced a great amount of relief, pleasure and "knowing." On Monday, I went into my boss's office and said, "I've decided to resign to live my dreams." I gave her a two-month notice and planned my dream work and worked my plan. The last two months of employment were daunting. I wanted to leave, and they wanted me to leave. They didn't want me challenging their beliefs and actions and bringing to the surface how they were not fulfilling the mission of the organization. It was evident how much I was valued and appreciated, and I vowed to never give my gifts away to anyone who did not appreciate them. I learned valuable lessons in my employment history, but I learned the most rewarding lessons in the three months prior starting my business. The greatest nugget of all was that it was more important to do work I love regardless of how much money I made. I thank God for enlightening me to move from a money focused way of living to a mission driven way of being.

This Soul Eruption, the chaos and craziness of this situation taught me a few thing: 1.) Money is not everything, 2.) Doing work you love is much more rewarding and fulfilling, and 3.) To put less focus on money and more emphasis on serving and sharing my gifts with the world. I've learned when you live on purpose your provisions will be met. I trust God more than ever to manage my bank account. I realize that I am the money, and I have the ability and gifts to create prosperity. I know for sure that answering and fulfilling my soul calling is more important than a six-figure income. I have arrived at this place because I mindfully mind my mindset, I don't allow my inner critic to have a front row seat in my life story, and I know how to turn my stinking thinking into power thoughts that produce the desires of my heart. I just do it afraid!

I regret nothing. All of the experiences leading up to this moment have shaped me into the woman I am and strive to become. My history has helped rise into resilience, leap into loving me as I am and courageously create the life I am living. When you own your mind and create your thoughts you create your life, create your destiny and create your legacy. My story is not unique; many women just like you chose to do work they love knowing when they genuinely serve the world from their heart the money will come.

What a bittersweet wakeup call! Let's flashback to my two jobs prior to 2005 when I officially filed my business name with the State of Nebraska: two consecutive job layoffs in a row. In retrospect, those were two big and obvious nudges telling me to use my gifts for my highest purpose. In a distant place, far away in my soul, I knew that to be true but was afraid to take the leap of faith. My soul *knew* it was time, and that there was a different path for me to travel, but I was afraid. I was afraid of the unknown, afraid of not having enough money to live the lifestyle I was use to, and afraid to fail.

FEAR is a liar! Fear told me that I could not survive the unknown in 2005. Today, I am not only surviving I AM thriving in this current moment. Fear had me believing I would not have enough money to live the lifestyle I want to live. Today, I'm living my dream free from having to get permission to use my natural gifts and the flexibility to *create my life on my terms*. Fear caused me to think I was going to fail. Today, I continue to overcome the fears I had all those years ago. Fear never goes away. It will be your destiny companion until you take your last breath. I've faced and overcame so many fears over the past ten years, and, as I look down the path to my destiny, I know fear is hiding in the bushes and following me along the way.

The job I spoke of in the previous excerpt required me to challenge myself in ways no other job before it had. My position as the Racial Justice Director certainly was a test of my soul's elasticity. For the first time in my professional career, I had the authority, "permission," and opportunity to *openly* talk about racism at work; not biases, diversity, oppression or discrimination, which are all watered down versions of the root problem of racism. Yeah man, I thought I hit the jackpot, but little did I know; my soul was about to become all jacked up! It started off great until I called out the hypocrisy of us pointing the finger at the community for not doing *enough* to end racism, while four fingers were pointing back at us. My adamant suggestion for us to challenge our own internal racism issues was initially encouraged but certainly not digested well when I started serving up the naked truth about what needed to be done to end racism.

I was committed to making a difference, but my body wasn't having it. My soul was feeling the stress of the work in a predominately white organization. At first, the staff would at least sample the appetizers of anti-racism education I offered them. It was mandatory they sit at the training table and eat at least one helping of eliminating racism education. A few of them gobbled it up, whereas most of them just picked at their plate and refused to get full. As time went on, most of the staff stopped coming to the table, and quite a few refused to even come into the dining room.

I reached the end of my rope! My soul was screaming stop! My body was rebelling with Irritable Bowel Syndrome and cold sores on my lips. At that fork in the road of my life, my soul was clearly and blatantly telling me *this is not your path; this is not the way.* I listened. I surrendered to the calling of my soul. That was it! Without an official and strategic plan, I finally said "yes" to my valuing my wisdom, my gifts, my talents and skill... I said "yes" to my significance! I made a promise to myself that I would "say yes" to my purpose and walk out my destiny no matter how afraid I was or what obstacles I encountered along the way. I also made another big promise to myself.

There is one promise I made to myself about seven years ago, a magical one! One that gave me the courage and inspiration to hop on my magic carpet and take the adventure of a life time, and I am still enjoying the ride. I made a promise I would completely and fully let go of the past and all that it included. This didn't mean that I totally forgot about everything that has ever happened to me, yet it meant I no longer allowed the past events of my life to determine the quantity and quality of my life to be determined by my past.

I promised I would not blame those who hurt me because I allowed the hurt to linger and manifest. I promised I would not relive the past because it was stealing my joy. I promised I wouldn't hold grudges against those who hurt me, deceived me, lied to me and or took me for granted. I realized while I was holding on and keeping my life captive, they had moved on and were enjoying life as if we never met. I promised myself I would allow healing to pour over my wounds because I *deserved* to be free of misery, worry and pain. I promised myself I would put myself first, forgive myself and love myself unconditionally with absolutely no strings attached. I made this *magical promise* to myself because I got sick and tired of being sick and tired and I knew I deserved better and more.

Over the past ten years, I've done what I call "*pulling weeds and planting seeds*." I uprooted all the weeds (people, places, events, obligations, feelings, thoughts, etc.) that keep me from seeing the beauty in my garden, my life. Pulling weeds and planting seeds allowed me to be very clear on what's important and focus on that which I desire to give energy to. When you *choose* to make the magical promise to yourself, you will find yourself in a similar situation that requires you to make difficult but necessary choices. You'll begin to mindfully choose who you trust and share space with. You'll choose who gets the honor of sitting in the front row of your life show. You'll choose how you spend your time and learn how to teach other people to respect it.

> Maybe it's time for you to make some promises and to pull some weeds and plant some seeds. Your soul's been whispering to you. You hear the voice. Listen to it. It knows the way. It always does.

You are not here by accident. There is a reason you are here. And every day you wake up to a new day, it is God's way of saying, *"Here's another opportunity for you to live out your purpose."* When you wake up in the morning, really think about the *potency* of that truth. I mean think deeply about it, and make a choice to "say yes" to your destiny. Every day is another chance to be significant. One of the most significant actions you can take right now is to own your life and every aspect of it. Do you own every part of your life? Are you taking responsibility for your thoughts, feelings, and behaviors? Here are six signs that you do NOT own your entire life.

6 Signs That You Are NOT Owning Your Life

1. You are stuck in the past and failing to create your now and tomorrow.

2. You are blaming other people for the current status of your life.

3. You are letting other people determine how your life should be lived.

4. You are waiting for the approval of others to make decisions and choices in your life.

5. You are contemplating everything about your life.

6. You are stuck in place and not moving forward towards your dreams.

Changing how you think and thinking about your thinking (Metacognition) is always the first and best place to start owning your life. Stinking thinking will always derail your destiny. Unleashing your significance requires you to think, choose and act. If you're stuck, lost, apathetic, ready to be more convicted about your purpose or want to amplify your significance, start with your thoughts. How much stinking thinking is controlling your life and creating detours on your destiny journey? Take a look at this checklist and determine how much stinking thinking is stealing your joy.

Stinking Thinking Thoughts That Keep You Stuck

_____You make a big deal out of trivial things.

_____You have the tendency to exaggerate your thoughts and blow them out of proportion.

_____Your thoughts tend to come from one end of the thought continuum or the other (right or wrong, good or bad and or black or white).

_____You fail to see the middle ground or grey area in your thoughts or the thoughts of others.

_____You worry about things happening before they do and with little evidence that they will.

_____You generalize everything, and your favorite words are never and always.

_____You have a hard time seeing and accepting other people's perspectives.

_____You think you know what people are thinking and make assumptions about people.

_____You're constantly thinking the worst things will happen.

_____You fail to see small successes and focus on the negative.

_____You think the world revolves around you, and, fail to see and appreciate the experiences of others.

_____You often think about who is bigger, better, smarter and richer.

_____You think your job, lack of finances, and or friends and family are the reason you are frustrated, unhappy or miserable.

_____You believe people don't appreciate you, and, if they would, your life would be better.

_____You think your self-sacrificing behaviors will eventually pay off when people realize your value.

_____You blame the world or yourself for the circumstances in your life.

_____You often use statements that include: I should, I could, I must, I need, and or I ought to.

_____You desire to be right and have no problem telling others when they are wrong.

Well... how much stinking thinking are you choosing to engage in? I have thought like this too many times to even begin to discuss. And, every day I have to be intentional about how I think. I am still guilty of stinking thinking every now and then, and I know my ego (Edging God Out) will always create opportunities to suck me into self-pity and sabotage. Yet, I have the power to own my thoughts and choose to think differently and so do you. A prerequisite to walking in your significance is taking ownership of your thoughts, feelings, behaviors and life. Here are five actions you can take right now to begin owning your life.

5 Things You Can Do Right Now to Begin Owning Your Life

1. Begin to forgive yourself. Forgive yourself for the mistakes you've made, the people you've hurt, the lies you've told, and all the other things that brought you pain or pain to others.

2. Forfeit in the game of blame. Get up from the game, walk away, and never play the game again. If you do, you are guaranteed to lose. It's your life; own it!

3. Make the magical promise to yourself and stick to it. You deserve it, your family and relationships deserve it. Everybody wins when you

make the magical promise. Refuse to make excuses. Excuses are the doorway to failure and lack of fulfillment.

4. Decide what you want and courageously go after it. Move from thinking about your dream and start living your dream, right now. You can be successful right where you are and by being who you are in this moment. Don't wait for everything to be perfect; take steps in the dark, and follow your soul's voice.

5. Get yourself out of the way. Do not allow your inner critic to talk you out of your goals, dreams and aspirations. Get in the driver's seat, and choose where you are going, how you will get there, who is going on the journey and who is staying behind, and fill the trunk with everything you need to create; BE significant because you matter, and YOU ARE SIGNIFICANT!

You, right now just as you are; own it. It's YOUR life; own it! Your life is yours and no one else's; take responsibility for who you are, who you become, how you think, what you do, the choices you make and the steps you take. Trust yourself. You can do this. Be still and listen to your soul's voice. It knows the way. It *always* knows the way!

"There's a voice that doesn't use words, listen to it." – Unknown

I MATTER
I AM
SIGNIFICANT

How have you been comparing your life to the lives of others?

_____

_____

_____

_____

Who are some people you know who show up, serve and or live a life you desire to live?

_____

_____

_____

_____

If you reach out to them and ask for support, what is it that you need from them?

_____

_____

_____

_____

When are you most inspired?

_____

_____

_____

_____

Can you hear the undeniable messages of your soul? Why or Why not?

_____

_____

_____

_____

In what ways are you dimming your light?

_____

_____

_____

_____

What would your life be like if you said a full body "yes" to your significance?

_____

_____

_____

_____

In what ways have you been money-focused and money driven?

_____

_____

_____

_____

What's your big mission in life?

_____

_____

_____

_____

How can you become more mission driven?

_____

_____

_____

_____

Fear is a liar! How has fear lied to you?

_____

_____

_____

_____

What physical symptoms are you experiencing that are telling you it's time to let something go and move on?

_____

_____

_____

_____

How are you owning your life?

_____

_____

_____

_____

In what ways are you NOT owning your life?

_____

_____

_____

_____

"Believe and act as if it were impossible
to fail."

– Charles Kettering

CHAPTER 5

Chapter 5

Tap Into Your Full Potential – Unlock Your Calling

ACTIVATE BELIEF

"Magic is believing in yourself. If you can do that, you can make anything happen." – Johann Wolfgang von Goethe

When you start hearing and responding to *the voice with no words* (your soul), that's when magic begins to unfold! The soul never speaks in "should," and it doesn't shame you into thinking or doing anything. Your soul's main agenda is to help you remember who you are, to remind you why you are here, and to keep you on the path of your purpose. Although, sometimes the voice of your soul can be loud or strong, it's *never* laced with *any* variation of fear. So that means feelings like doubt, worry, jealousy, or anger are *not* in the soul's vocabulary. Those feelings are the language of your ego. *Your soul is divine*. It's the bridge between you and God; it *only* speaks the language of love.

Your ego, however, is masterfully designed to serve as your protector. It's your built in alarm system; it's a caution voice. It does speak the language of doubt, worry, fear, jealousy and anger. That's exactly what it is supposed to do. Your ego is a psychological construct, a defense mechanism that sits right in the middle of your fight or flight response. When you feel threatened or angry, the ego is ready to take action to defend and protect you at all cost. The ego speaks like this: *"say something so you don't look stupid, don't invest in that you can't afford it, don't trust them they're going to hurt you, tell them off and cuss them out before they do it to you,"* and various other phrases laced with fear.

One of the easiest ways to determine which voice you listen to the most is by examining your thoughts, feelings and behaviors. If you've got a lot of stinking thinking going on, you tend to be more sad or aggravated than happy and peaceful, and or you are lashing out and arguing more than you are calmly engaging with others then you're listening more to the voice of your ego. It's not complicated. Pay attention to how you think, feel and engage, and you'll find your answer. Love feels good and fear does not. This is one mindfulness technique I'm still learning to master. Mastery becomes possible when you live in the present moment and respond more than you react to your circumstances.

> Remember, your soul's voice is the bridge between you and your creator; therefore, the soul's voice speaks the language of love, hope, faith, forgiveness, understanding, empathy and grace. Your soul wants you to experience all the goodness possible!

Let's dig one layer deeper into fully understanding your ego and why it's critical you know its purpose and plan for your life. The ego is inherently helpful in some ways. The ego is a part of how you define yourself and gives you the energy and drive to survive and thrive in life. If you've ever heard someone say that people act on their own *free will*, essentially their ego is running the show. To help give you a visual, picture a ladder. At the top of the ladder is what's called the *self*, your *higher will;* the part of you that is divinely connected to God and others. The self, in other words, is your soul. At the bottom of the ladder is your ego. Your ego is connected to your *lower will,* or the part of you that naturally strives for power, competition, security and survival. The ladder itself is your personality.

Your personality is like a container. It is the external shell that encompasses your *higher will* (self) and your *lower will* (ego). The way you think, feel and behave is your personality and your overall psyche. Creativity and humor, for example, are parts of your personality. On a day to day basis, most people show the world their ego and personality. For example, when I describe a person as a single mother who works in a factory as a supervisor who is charming, talkative and very competitive, I am essentially describing her ego and personality. The roles you play and how you show up and present yourself are more often the representation of your ego and personality at play. Your *true self, your higher will, your soul* does NOT need "roles" to play and are your purest essence. It is in this divine essence that your "calling" or purpose lies.

When you are alone (or with others) and not trying to prove yourself or put on, you are acting as your true self. When you have every reason to tell someone off when they've offended you and you don't, you are acting as your higher self. When your circumstances or the evidence you see in your life dictates that you should be worried but you are at peace inside, your soul is leading the way. When you move through the world unmoved by drama, unbothered by other people's opinions and behaviors and with a sense of direction, knowing and peace, you are moving with and towards purpose. THIS is the sweet spot! When you behave like this, you are being your most divine, magnificent self.

Think back to chapter two when I described myself with I AM statements. That was my attempt to describe to you who I believe I AM in my purest most divine form. Even I have difficulty truly describing what it means to be a soul because your soul is so divine there are often few words to describe something so pure, perfect and transcendent. Why? Because that is the part of us that is most God-like. I do know this for sure; the self (your soul) is not a role, a title, a possession or even a physical characteristic. When we go down the wrong paths in life, lash out in fits of rage and or fall into the pit of pity and despair, our egos led the way, not our souls.

The ego is a forever companion on this journey called life, and it can be difficult to distinguish the difference between its voice and the voice of our higher selves, our soul. Yet, we must be very intentional in every moment to learn and know the difference if we want to live out the destiny of our lives. Three of the ego's best tricks for sabotage are creating diversions, distractions and rationalization. Diversions and distractions show up in everyday life like the husband who works late on purpose to avoid coming home to what he calls a "nagging" wife. Abusing alcohol or drugs is a way to avoid dealing with life's challenges. The ego says this behavior is okay; it justifies it and helps rationalize behavior that is clearly unhelpful or destructive.

Ultimately, when you operate and show up in life leading with your ego, (blame, doubt, lying, telling partial truths, bragging, plotting, scheming, worrying, abusing substances, and or deceit), you take a detour from your highest self, your soul's calling and a life of integrity and purpose. People who just get by, settle and make ends meet in life are being led by their ego, and most of them don't even know it. If you're living that kind of life now, and yet, feel that something is missing or there's an internal conflict in what you want and what you're experiencing, there is a battle happening within between your soul and your ego. Who is winning? Listen to your soul if you want to win!

Your ego is a powerful part of who you are, and while it serves to help you in many ways, it is also your greatest adversary. The cartoon image of the devil on one shoulder and the angel on the other shoulder is real. It's not as fictional as you'd like to believe. You are experiencing on a daily basis the struggle between leading with your ego and leading with your soul. Which one is in charge of your life right now? When the battle ensues, which one is more victorious? I'm going out on a limb to say that if you have not answered your call, are not living out your purpose, and or living a life of significance, your ego is winning! It doesn't have to be the victor; you can with daily awareness, metacognition and intentional choices choose to let your soul win! I fight a good fight every day! I will be victorious and so will you.

You're going to make mistakes. Ego is going to win sometimes. You will fall short. Today is your wakeup call! Any mistakes, victories of the ego and shortcomings you've experienced in the past may have been a part of not knowing what you know now. It's true. You don't know what you don't know. Yet, once you know something and you choose to ignore it or act upon your own free will, then you are choosing your own self-destruction and demise. I hope this psychological lesson has awakened you into a new, higher level of consciousness. I hope now, when you begin to participate in stinking thinking, fall into the pity pit and or begin to worry or blame others for your feelings, you'll realize who is running the show. And, if you continue to let your ego lead the way, you create detours that delay your destiny.

I am not immune to the detours and delays orchestrated by the ego. I fall short often, sometimes daily. I'm on the battlefield for my life. I'm fighting in every second to live my purpose, let my soul lead the way and be significant in the world. Every day I am awakened to the possibilities and outcomes that occur by choosing to listen to my soul's voice and allow it to reign in my life. Some days and moments my soul wins, and other times it does not. Yet, every single day I wake up I know I have the choice to choose the ego's way or my soul's way. I also know there is more for me to know, be, and do in the world, and every day I seek it out. Why? Because I know I AM here to complete my divine assignment. One of my daily declarations is *"God use me to my greatest capacity and to my fullest potential."*

LIVING YOUR FULL POTENTIAL BY LEANING INTO FEAR

When you lean into something you first know, "it" is present; you have a conscious awareness that it exists. The "it" I'm referring to in this case is FEAR. I must admit; answering your soul's calling is scary and full of uncertainty. Sometimes the fear emerges because you don't know *what* the call is, and, often times, you're afraid because you don't know (or believe) whether you can carry it out. I've been afraid for both reasons in the past, and today there are still traces of fear related to not knowing or believing I can fulfill such a big call. This feeling of fear I experience is a sure sign I can hear my unique calling; otherwise, I would not feel fear. Fear shows its face *only* when you are about to step out of your comfort zone, when you move into a dimension that's unfamiliar, and or when you step outside of what you've mastered.

If you asked me to write a ten-page paper on what is love, I could easily and effortlessly write it quickly with very little tension. If you asked me to then present my information to a group of one hundred people in person, I could easily and excitedly do it with a fraction of tension in the first couple of minutes. If you asked me to explain the quantitative power of love in a mathematical equation, I would freeze up, become mentally paralyzed and more than likely not be able to accomplish it. Why? Because words come easy for me, I'm a natural wordsmith, I have the gift of voice, and I'm an excellent communicator. I'm very comfortable writing, speaking and teaching because I have mastered those skills. On the other hand, I have not mastered algebra or any other mathematical concepts and skills beyond basic addition, subtraction, multiplication and division, and I don't plan on it!

Thank God my purpose doesn't involve solving difficult mathematical problems because numbers and equations are way outside of my comfort zone. When I'm presented with or forced to face mathematical situations, fear rises up in my belly like a great beast and takes over. I become anxious and confused, and my brain either shuts down or starts stirring up stinking thinking. Can you relate? Is there a certain topic, issue, place, person or space that ignites the fear within you? What I've described is typical *fear of the unknown*.

There's another kind of fear called *positive fear*. Let's say I'm experiencing fear around mathematical equations, and I begin to think *"what will people think of me"* or *"what are people going to say about my lack of knowledge?"* Since being a math genius is NOT my calling, this type of stinking think has no real relevance but is very normal; this is an example of *positive* fear. My ego knows I am out of my comfort zone, and it's trying to protect me. However, if my calling is to set the lives of hurting people free and this kind of stinking thinking rises up, it is absolutely relevant because my ego is trying to talk me out of walking in my destiny.

When you begin answering your call, fear and stinking thinking shows up exactly when you know you need or want to do something to expand your greatness. It emerges when you step outside of your comfort zone and becomes more intense with every step you take in the direction to act on your call. It's important to know the difference between the type of fear you experience as you navigate through life. "Typical" fear thoughts produced by the ego are generally designed to keep you safe; positive fear is designed to talk you out of your destiny. Think about it this way; when your ego tries to talk you out of taking the risk to be greater, it's a reminder to just do it. See this type of fear as a positive nudge to move forward even though you may be scared as hell.

Your true calling may be foreign to you. Your soul call may be way outside your comfort zone. Your purpose and divine assignment may be so big or profound that you're not sure the call is for you and or that you have the container to carry the call or the capacity to carry it out. Your calling may require that you start giving up what was familiar and comfortable to make space for the unknown. It may put you in places you never imagined you'd be. I'm sure it will do all of this. *Your call is not about you.* Your call is not about awards, accolades and achievements. Your call may not bring you immense pleasure. Your call is for the world.

Dr. Martin Luther King, Jr.'s call was bittersweet as he experienced quite a bit of anguish, despair and pain while fulfilling his destiny. He didn't answer the call for a Nobel Peace Prize; he answered the call to do his part to usher in peace and harmony during an ugly and hateful time in our history.

Your soul's voice will always nudge you about your call. It will whisper and sometimes shout at you to hear and answer it, and, while it may be startling, you know it's right for you. Your calling is bigger than you, and you'll never be able to fulfill it alone. Your calling or purpose may not have a definite ending. Your calling will require other people to help you carry it out. Take poverty for example. Do you know how long people have been suffering from and fighting to end poverty? Since the beginning of time essentially, and is poverty still a burdensome human condition? It sure is! Imagine if eliminating poverty was a purpose that belonged to no one. Just imagine the state or condition people would be in had there not been people called to eliminate poverty.

You may be thinking if poverty will never end and why would people be called to address it. I don't have an answer, but I do pose a question for you. What would the state of humanity look like if no one since the beginning of time ever fought to eliminate poverty? What kind of lives would people live today? The intention for answering your call is for you to be in service to the call and to make your unique contribution to the vision and ideals of a mission for the elevation of humanity. Think about how many people in the world are fighting to end cancer. There is no cure yet. Imagine if we adopted the belief that those with cancer are going to die anyway so why try?

True soul callings may be never ending. You may play a vital role in the activation and progression of a cause but may not necessarily be the one to fulfill it or be there to see the victory. Don't let the grandiosity of "callings" scare you away from answering yours. Yes your work here on earth is related to some human cause, but it may not be yours alone to solve or eliminate. And, if it is something you can accomplish all by yourself, it's not your true calling but rather a goal with a clear ending that you've created for yourself. *Goals may be about you but callings never are.* Remember, we are here to love and serve. Answering your call is your service to the world.

When you begin hearing your call clearer and answering it, *positive* fear and stinking thinking will increase. That's when you lean in, acknowledge it, know that your ego is doing its job, and then begin to tune it out and dial in to the frequency of your soul voice. Fear is simply the part of your internal navigation system that warns you that you are about to stretch outside of your comfort zone. That's why it's been said, *feel the fear and do it anyway!* Feel it and keep moving your feet. Take one step if you have to and pause. Take the step, and then listen for the soul voice to speak. If the soul voice says, "*that was scary but keep going, you're going the right way, and you can do this, take another step.*" Pause. Listen. Step forward!

HOW TO BEGIN TO UNLOCKING YOUR CALL

For everything that is gained, there will be a loss. For every step forward, you'll leave something (or someone) behind. For every action, there will be a reaction, and, for every choice, there will be a positive or negative consequence. There's no way around this. It is the ebb and flow of life and the natural, logical consequence of choice. As you begin to unlock your unique calling, you will lose, people will react negatively, and you may endure some negative consequences. It's part of the process, the plan and the purpose of you being here. Acknowledge it, accept it and keep moving forward in spite of it. Answering your call, living out your purpose, fulfilling your destiny, and being significant will not always be a happy, sparkly, party ride.

I want you to be significant in the world, and it begins by tapping into your potential, discovering your purpose and answering your call. By the time you finish reading this book, maybe you'll know what your purpose of call is, but it's unlikely because it can take time. Nevertheless, let's begin the search because tomorrow is not promised, so let's seize this moment. You may already know what pulls on your heart strings, what keeps you up at night, what makes your heart hurt or the conditions of the human spirit that speak to your empathetic self. Maybe you also know what excites you, makes your heart sing or what causes you to feel fully alive inside. And, if you don't, the following exercise may wake these things up inside of you.

Read the following statements below, and then fill in the blank with the answer that comes from your heart and soul not your mind or ego. No one is going to see this but you so be completely honest in your response. Let's get started.

DISCOVERING WHAT MATTERS TO YOUR SOUL

I love_____

I am passionate about_____

I feel compassion toward_____

The greatest tragedy would be_____

I would really love to_____

I am enthused when_____

The most meaningful thing is _____

I am inspired by_____

I come alive when _____

I like to think about_____

I wonder why_____

If I could change one thing in the world, it would be_____

The most important thing in my life is_____

I value this most _____

My deepest wish is_____

I am most capable of _____

I have a special ability to _____

My greatest talent is _____

I would do this for free_____

I admire _____

I need this to feel complete_____

My dream job or career is _____

This gives me satisfaction_____

I desire this to be happy_____

This person would be a great mentor for me_____

I am willing to take a risk on _____

The vision for my life is _____

People say I am good at_____

People describe me as _____

I feel compelled to _____

It is right to _____

I feel connected to _____

I am creative when _____

My heart feels for _____

I wish the world were more_____

My heart hurts when_____

It saddens me to see people_____

If I had a million dollars, I would_____

I would love to donate my time to_____

I place high value on_____

Now that you've completed this exercise, what are you thinking? How do you feel? Go back for a few moments and look at your responses. Look closely, and see if you can see any themes or responses that are similar. Look for the repetition of certain words. See if you can find a certain demographic of people you have a heart for. Check again to see if you can determine what excites you and makes you feel energized. Lastly, go back and find the human condition (struggle, issue or problem) that your heart says, "*yes I would love to help/serve those people*." What do you see? This list is not conclusive. There are so many other questions you can ask yourself to begin to discover what you are here to do and who you are meant to serve.

Don't stop with the process of asking questions and listening for answers. Whatever higher power you believe in, ask for the answers to be revealed to you through every medium possible. Here's what I mean. I can be on social media and see posts and comments that immediately grab my attention, and my soul whispers *"that's for you; it's part of your path."* I can be watching television and certain shows or commercials cause my soul to say, *"that's part of your purpose; what will you do about it?"* I can be amongst strangers in an airport, and, while I'm people watching, a certain someone or situation evokes a message from my soul that says, *"pray for them, or they need help."* My soul isn't saying, *"this is how you do it"* but rather *"you are here to do something about it."* And most times, my soul doesn't speak actual words, but I get this indescribable *knowing* of familiarity in my spirit.

Not all soul nudges are soft or feel exceptionally *good*. Here's what I mean. I know one of the biggest human problems (conditions) I'm here to address, solve or transform is racism and specifically related to women. For as long as I can remember, my eyes and soul have been keenly tuned into the racial injustices in the world. I've experienced racism intimately, and I know the devastating effects it can create emotionally, psychologically and physically in the lives of the recipients. Acts of racism, big or small, intentional or unintentional hurt, wound and oppress people and leave lasting psycho-spiritual scars. Talking about racism, advocating against racism and doing activist work is terrifying, challenging, exhausting, and, at the same time, inspiring, liberating, affirming, and satisfying. *"It hurts so good"* would be perfect words to describe my calling. It's bittersweet.

Callings of course can contain more elements of joy, happiness and delight. You don't have to dread your calling nor does it have to be emotionally laborious. Just know that when you say "yes" to a calling or purpose, there will be some bitter sweetness in the mix. That is exactly the way it is supposed to be. And, you don't answer the call once and then it's over. You courageously keep answering your call every day. The intention is to fully live out your purpose and complete your divine assignment until you take your last breath. Lastly, consider that you may have more than one calling in your lifetime. Don't worry about it; just answer it, do your part and be significant. And while you're at it, make time to live, love, laugh, play, relax and enjoy life as much as you possibly can!

A SUGGESTION FOR THE JOURNEY

You're sure to experience challenges, face obstacles and encounter many doubters and naysayers when you answer your calling, but your soul will be happy, and your heart and mind will *know* you are doing the right thing for humanity. This is exactly why you have to seek out and hang out with other destiny seekers, purpose pushers and significance junkies. They will get it. They will understand your conviction about the perceived craziness you said "yes" to. They will support you, and you will support them. The vision won't sound delusional to them. They will understand *why* your calling wakes you up early and keeps you up late. These are your purpose people, and, if you're ready to say "yes" to your calling and be significant, it's time you go find them. You need them. They need you. They are waiting for you!

> *"Believe in yourself. Believe in your calling, and go out and make magic happen." – Catrice M. Jackson*

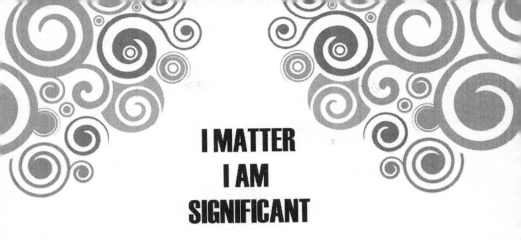

I MATTER
I AM
SIGNIFICANT

How do you know when the voice of your soul is speaking?

_____
_____
_____
_____

In what ways do you lead with your ego?

_____
_____
_____
_____

What do you think your soul's calling is?

_____
_____
_____
_____

What do you desire that is outside of your comfort zone?

_____
_____
_____
_____

What are you willing to lose to gain everything you desire?

_____

_____

_____

_____

Who are the doubters and naysayers in your life?

_____

_____

_____

_____

Who are the destiny seekers in your life?

_____

_____

_____

_____

What do you need to believe in order to go out and create magic in your life?

_____

_____

_____

_____

"I am homesick for a place I am not sure even exists. One where my heart is full. My body loved. And my soul understood."

— Melissa Cox

CHAPTER 6

Chapter 6

Money, Meaning and Making a Difference

ACTIVATE MEANING

"Life is not measured by the number of breaths we take, but by the moments that take our breath away." – Unknown

You have the potential to be, do and experience more! Whatever *more* means for you, you can have it when you tap into your greatest potential. Your *more* may include a better job, more money, a nicer home, vibrant health and or a loving relationship. Maybe your *more* is a retirement fund, a summer home, exotic adventures or traveling the world. Some people frown upon the notion of wanting more or better and would rather *"be grateful for what they have"* or *settle* for what they have and that's totally cool with me. But, I know *who* I belong to. I know who my heavenly father is, and I know that I AM an heir to his riches. I *choose* to believe I can have all that I desire, and that it's already prepared and waiting for me. What about you? What do you believe?

I didn't always believe I was an heir to God's riches. In fact, especially surrounding money, I wasn't taught to even desire large amounts of money because *"money was the root of all evil."* Did you ever hear that growing up? What about *"money doesn't grow on trees?"* Yep, I was told that over and over as a kid and young adult. The subject of wealth and prosperity weren't even discussed in my family. I honestly don't even think I ever heard the words used at all. No doubt we were financially poor and spiritually rich. It was well into my early thirties before I became curious to explore wealth and prosperity. I was thirty-six to be exact. I specifically remember the book that opened my eyes to the possibilities of financial abundance.

Sometimes I search for certain books, and other times books search for and find me. In a serendipitous moment in the bookstore back in 2007, I was looking for a particular personal development book. An interesting book with a beautiful and captivating cover jumped out at me. I picked up the book, flipped through the pages and was immediately drawn in by the title *Creating Money: Keys to Abundance*. I did not hesitate. I bought the book, forgot about the one I was actually looking for and went home to dive in. I had no idea just how deep I was about to dive. My mind was blown within reading the first couple of paragraphs. For the first time in my life, I heard and believed that I AM the money, and I CAN create money.

YOUR GIFTS WILL MAKE ROOM FOR YOU AND MONEY TOO

Let me connect the dots for you. Being led to this book was no accident. Remember, I told you I left my job to create my dream in 2008. The Divine One already knew; my soul already knew; I was going to need this information way before I realized it. This is why I know for sure the book found me. Prior to reading this book, I was a skimmer. I had never read a book cover to cover. I was too impatient to sit still and would easily get bored. This book was different. It drew me in from front to back and I couldn't wait to get off work and open up this treasure chest of brilliance. I had a dramatic new perspective about money, wealth, prosperity and abundance. And to sweeten the deal, for the first time, I discovered the *power of belief, intentionality and manifestation*.

Creating Money: Keys to Abundance was a captivating catalyst that inspired me to write my first book, *Soul Eruption!* If you've ever discovered eye-opening, life-changing information that upon applying it you transformed your life, you know exactly what I mean. What does this have to do with you? Is money stopping you from living your dream, starting a business, igniting a movement or saying "yes" to your calling? Have you envisioned a vision so big that you believe you need a lot of money to make it a reality? Having money or an abundance of money certainly does create more inner peace and security. One of the greatest lessons I learned on this journey called the life of an entrepreneur is that, *I AM the money, and I CAN create money!*

Not too long ago while listening to an audio sermon shared by T.D. Jakes, Pastor and New York Times Best-Selling Author, I was reminded of this truth that I AM the money. He said, *"as long as you have gifts, you're never broke."* Oh my gosh! When I heard those words, I got excited again about the possibilities to move my mission forward in faith at a time when the finances were not readily available. Do you truly get the depth and divineness of this statement? If we keep it simple, your true source of abundance lies within you and not in external institutions. This is exactly how millions of people turn the fire in their belly into bank signs every day. They are entrepreneurs, authors, artists, business owners, consultants, freelancers, musicians, comedians, chefs, and coaches.

At some point in all of these people's lives, they realized and believed their gifts *would* make room for them. They longed to express their ideas and explore the curiosity of what lies within. They said "yes" to the nagging desire to activate all of the glorious, multi-dimensional magic dying to be unleashed inside. They fed their insatiable hunger to escape the rules, red tape and regulations required when you *have to* do it someone else's way. Turning the fire in your belly into bank signs is not always glamorous. When you choose to manifest your dreams and live out your purpose, there *will* be some pain and problems on the path. There will be frustration and fear, yet with faith, focus and the refusal to faint, you *will* produce and taste the fruit of your gifts.

Your calling may not be like those with the *entrepreneurial* spirit. It may be within an organization, a company or in the community, and, even so, your gifts will *still* make room for you. In other words, you can use your divine gifts within an established sphere and still answer your call, be on purpose, and make a difference. It doesn't necessarily matter *where* you use your gifts; it's more important that you *choose* to use your gifts for the greater good of humanity.

> Are you using your divine gifts, in the right place, for the right purpose, with the right people?

Regardless of where you are using them, do you feel broke? By broke, I mean, do you feel like you are working hard, barely making it and unfulfilled? Or perhaps you're working hard, making good money and you're still unfulfilled. And, maybe you're doing work you love, making good money but not making the impact and difference in the world you'd like to.

What I'm trying to say is you can have it all: *money, meaning and making a difference*. When I was working full time, I earned plenty of money. My needs were met, my bills were paid, and there was enough money left over for savings and fun. Also, while working full time for someone else, I was *never* completely fulfilled. I was always a stellar employee and enjoyed my work, but I've never had a job that I could call *my purpose*. I never had a job that made me leap out of bed in the morning and stay up late at night. I always knew each job was a stepping stone and lesson for the path I am on today. I AM grateful for every job I had, yet, I knew deep down inside there was something *more* for me to experience.

7 SIGNS THAT TOLD ME THERE WAS MORE TO EXPERIENCE

1. Once I mastered the duties and improved the program, I was bored.

2. There were days I dreaded going and couldn't wait to leave.

3. I always felt like I was expected to minimize my natural strengths because shining too bright was not easily accepted by my co-workers.

4. I felt like having plenty of money was NOT enough.

5. I only seemed to be able to stay at one job for a certain amount of time.

6. I often felt like I could be a better leader than my leader.

7. I felt like I wasn't allowed to fully utilize all of my gifts. I was only walking in partial greatness.

8. All in all, I realized I was sacrificing my health, happiness, creativity, and brilliance to avoid being broke. I reached a point where I refused to dim my light to keep colleagues comfortable. I felt a sense of urgency to fulfill my destiny. I craved freedom, flexibility and total control over my life. I desired to leave a legacy that my children and children's children could own. My vision for my life was screaming to be unleashed! I didn't want to die full with my hopes and dreams still inside of me. I desperately wanted to make a difference in the world, in my own way without having to follow someone else's rules. It was time to walk into my destiny, and I *did it afraid* because my soul needed and deserved *money, meaning and making a difference.*

I'm not telling you to leave your job or to become an entrepreneur. I AM encouraging you to dare to believe you can make money, do meaningful work and make a difference in the world. How you define money, meaning and making a difference is up to you. There are no rules. There is no prescription, template, formula or blueprint that works for everyone. It's your life, your calling, your purpose and your destiny. What I do know is unleashing your significance in the sphere of your choosing and calling *is* the way to have all three!

7 SIGNS IT MAY BE TIME FOR YOU TO LEAVE YOUR JOB TO EXPERIENCE MORE

1. You don't consistently feel deeply passionate or excited about the work you do.

2. You dread going to work and don't like your boss or colleagues.

3. Work-related issues are causing you to experience physical symptoms or emotional stress.

4. You don't believe in the mission or vision, and you're staying just to make money.

5. You are not productive, giving your best, or crave to do work that excites and fulfills you.

6. Your best skills are not being used, your ideas don't get heard, and or you feel like you're just going through the motions.

7. You're bored and or don't see yourself doing this work for the rest of your life.

8. When you think about your job or work, does any of this resonate with you? When you think about going to work on Monday, does any of this bubble up in your belly? Is there a voice or whisper that tells you that you need more or deserve more? Don't ignore the voice! *It's your soul's voice, and it always knows the way.* Far too many times we settle in life for a variety of reasons. We don't know we are settling. We've been taught to settle. Stepping outside of our comfort zone is easier than taking the risk to experience more. We don't know what we want or what more will look like. We're afraid to fail at seeking more. We've been made to believe that wanting more is being ungrateful. If you want more and have been thinking about having more, does any of this sound familiar?

What if more was expansive and limitless? What would your more look like? THIS is the perfect time for you to dream the grandest dream your mind can create, and then choose to make it a reality. You deserve more. I deserve more. Deserving and the ability to *believe* you deserve is a mental muscle that must be strengthened every day. A good friend of mine teaches about *raising your deserve level.* Your deserve level is like an invisible line you've drawn in your mind that determines how much goodness and splendor you will allow yourself to have. The invisible psychological line also determines how much you will put up with or settle for. Is your deserve level high or low? *Here's a quick and easy way to see how high or low it is. Put a check mark by the statements that most often apply to your life.*

_____ I feel more overwhelmed than I feel in control.

_____ I experience more worry or doubt than I feel confidence.

_____ I feel heavy and bogged down more than I feel energized.

_____ I feel overworked and undercompensated.

_____ I feel stuck more than I feel like I'm moving forward.

_____ I feel unappreciated often by those I love.

_____ I often think I could have a better job or bring more money into my business.

_____ I feel awkward or uncomfortable when people give me gifts or compliments.

_____ I often attract negative or toxic people in my life.

_____ I frequently wonder when it's going to be my turn.

_____ I know I'm in situations that don't feel good, but I don't take the steps to free myself.

_____ I often say or think, "something is better than nothing."

_____ I often envy other people's successes, relationships, careers or finances.

_____ I feel like I am settling in more than one area of my life.

If you are an entrepreneur or business owner, your deserve level matters in your line of work too. Boy, how I know this to be true. I remember the early days as an entrepreneur when family and friends thought I was crazy to leave a good paying job with benefits to chase a dream they could not see or understand. Sure, there was an element of crazy to the pursuit, but it's the crazy ones who believe they can change the world and often do. Besides, I proclaimed (and knew) I would become an entrepreneur at the naïve age of eighteen, even though I had no idea how I was going to make it happen.

Countless times I had to remind my family that although I was working in pajamas many days, I was *still* working. People would call me during the day and say, "*what are you doing?*" Uh, I'm working! They would call and ask for rides as if I had free time because I worked from home. In the early days of my entrepreneurial journey, I would do lots of things that indicated my deserve level was low. I would take on just about any client because I needed the money. I would dim my light in the space of the big-wig entrepreneurs. I was afraid to self-promote because I didn't want to seem too arrogant. I spent way too much time and energy worrying about what people might think which prevented me from having and experiencing what I DESERVED!

> Those days are over! I AM worthy. I matter. I AM significant and so are you.

Your deserve level is a combination of the internal images you have of yourself, your self-esteem, what you believe to be true about you and a culmination of the internal messages (beliefs) you have about yourself based on other people's opinions. This psycho-emotional concoction draws the deserve line in your mind, and, until you intentionally do the mental work to raise the line, you'll feel unworthy of what you really deserve. You can start now. Change won't happen overnight, but, with daily practice, you WILL raise your deserve level. And, until you raise it, you will continue to settle, and it will be difficult for you to create your "*more*" and enjoy it.

TIPS TO RAISE YOUR DESERVE LEVEL

- **Ask for help.** I suggest a licensed therapist or a mindset coach. Whomever you choose, they need to be someone objective who not only *sees, honors and celebrates* your significance but can help YOU see, honor and celebrate it. Be willing to be vulnerable. It is in vulnerability that you become humble, healed and happy.

- **Start forgiving and begin with you.** Holding grudges keeps you in captivity. Ever notice how the people you haven't forgiven are moving forward with and enjoying their lives? The only one brooding, harboring and feeling miserable is you. Forgiveness is a beautiful gift. Set you and others free. You can practice daily affirmations that

start with *"I now forgive myself {or the other person} for _____.*
I release it completely, and I am free and happy." Do this as many
times as necessary until you no longer hold a grudge.

- **Celebrate others.** It's easy to envy and be jealous of the success
  and possessions of others and it's pretty normal. When you see
  someone being, doing or having what you desire, pause and
  celebrate them. Feel the excitement with them and know that if they
  can be, do or have it so can you. ENERGY is everything. The more
  positive energy you put out into the world the more positivity you'll
  experience. **Don't think you are jealous envious of others? Next
  time someone shares great news or gets something new, notice
  how you FEEL. If you don't feel LOVE feelings… you are jealous
  or envious.**

- **Practice gratitude.** When you see your friends, family, and
  colleagues living or experiencing *their* more… be grateful for what
  you have. There are plenty of people in the world who wish they
  were you and or had what you have. Being grateful and expressing
  gratitude opens up the doors for you to receive *your* more.

- **Stop wishing and start doing your work.** If you don't get in the
  game, you'll never know if you can win. Don't be afraid to fail.
  Failure is part of the journey. Expect it because along the way it will
  happen. Failure is not losing. Failure is feedback that tells you to try
  something else and try again. When you fail, instead of thinking and
  saying things like, *"I suck. I'm no good. I'm never doing that again."*
  say *"I learned what did not work, or I learned how to do it better."*

- **Decide what you want.** Make a list of what you really want. Believe
  you deserve it all. Set some achievable yet flexible goals. Determine
  what you need and who you need to help you achieve the goals.
  Create a plan and get to work. Nothing works if you don't work it. If
  you're not seeing progress, check your beliefs and raise your deserve
  level. If you're not advancing forward, get advice from the people
  you asked to help you. If you're not yet experiencing your more,
  reassess your strategy and change it or add a different approach to

the plan. No matter what, don't quit! Be curious. Explore alternatives and other options. Be sure to celebrate *every* forward movement and success.

- Unleashing your significance and living a life that matters must have meaning. Are you living a meaningful life? What does meaning mean to you? By nature, we are selfish, self-serving human beings. We are wired to survive or die. It is in the relentless quest to survive that we often fail to appreciate who we are and how far we've come. I'm a naturally driven person, so the pursuit of success is in my genes. Once I set a goal, I usually don't need external motivation to accomplish it, unless of course, the goal is related to weight loss; then I could certainly use my own cheerleading squad. I'm working on it (smile).

I AM successful on my own terms, and in a lot of ways, according to the "standards of society," many would say I am successful. I've accomplished quite a bit and more than others I know. I'm a dissertation away from receiving my doctoral degree in Psychology. I have a Master's Degree in Counseling. I've successfully practiced mental health therapy for over fifteen years. I have a Bachelor's Degree in Criminal Justice. I'm a non-practicing Licensed Practical Nurse and Cosmetologist. I've written six books prior to this one, been an entrepreneur for nine years, lovingly raised my only son, and have been married for over fifteen years (a total of 23 years together). I'd say I am very successful.

While I'm proud of and grateful for my achievements and accomplishments, something was still missing. I've volunteered my time and talent many times, donated money to charities, mentored other women, given back to my community and hosted numerous empowerment events for women. All of this giving back felt good, yet it was fleeting. It felt good in the moment, but my soul kept longing for something deeper and long-lasting. Throughout the year 2015, I often silently and openly said, *"there's more for me be, do, experience and give in my lifetime."* Quite frankly, the driven woman within was becoming uninterested in pursuing success, tired of the hustle and grind, and *so* over all of the hype and dogma of what it means to be a *successful* entrepreneur.

Like I do every year, I meditated on what my ONE word would be for 2016. I asked God for guidance and for the word to be undeniably dropped into my spirit. I waited for the knowing to overtake me. And then, clearly I heard the word SIGNIFICANCE. I knew it was the *right* word for *this* season of my life, and it felt good. I said "yes" to the word and the intention of the word. What does significance mean to me? Significance, while meaning important, also means giving attention and time to what matters, focusing on what's important, and participating in things that are meaningful. I chose to be significant and think, live and give significantly.

Since choosing my one word, I've intentionally given my time, energy, focus and resources to people, situations and events that matter to me. I feel in total alignment with my soul's request, and I'm looking forward to all of the possibilities to be significant on the path of my purpose. I still have goals in place and strategies I'm implementing to succeed, but it feels so liberating and refreshing to exert focused energy into living significantly. I am here to love and to serve like you. In this time in my life, being of tremendous service to the world is in the forefront of my mind.

Have you reached a point in your life where service and significance is calling your name and becoming more audacious about it? Is the call getting clearer and louder? Have you too been chasing the success train and crave something deeper and more satisfying? Maybe it's time for you to discover and live out your own version of significance. Let's begin with this.

WHAT MATTERS MOST TO YOU?

WHAT WOULD MAKE YOUR LIFE MORE MEANINGFUL?

WHAT DOES LIVING A SIGNIFICANT LIFE LOOK LIKE FOR YOU?

HOW DO YOU WANT TO BE OF HIGHEST SERVICE TO THE WORLD?

SIMPLE WAYS TO MAKE A DIFFERENCE IN THE WORLD

- Love yourself–it will ripple into the lives of others.
- Be yourself–it will inspire others to do the same.
- Show up–it will empower others to take their place.
- Shine–it will encourage others to illuminate their brilliance.
- Smile–it's a universal language that's contagious.
- Make a difference in your own home first.
- Choose to be and spread love instead of fear.
- Forgive quickly and set yourself and others free.
- Honor your value and teach others how to treat you.
- Be with people who encourage you to be yourself.
- Practice Metacognition – think about your thinking.
- Be grateful – gratitude opens the door for you.
- Help as many people as you can without putting yourself last.
- Do something nice for someone anonymously.
- Be responsible for the energy you bring into the lives of others.
- Listen. Listen. Listen.
- Tell the people you love that you love them.
- Live your dream and show your children what's possible.

- Make choices not decisions.

- Make every moment count.

- Help someone else achieve their dream.

- Find at least one person you can mentor.

- Discover your gifts and give them away.

- Be intentional with your words and actions.

- *What's your purpose?* You are here to love and serve, and there's a unique way for you and only you to carry out your divine assignment. Loving you unapologetically and loving others unconditionally is where you begin. Love who you are, what you look like and every single imperfect thing about you. *Don't settle for mundane work.* Tap into what makes you feel alive inside, and make that your life's work. *Don't settle for mediocrity.* Discover what you deeply desire, and spend your time and energy creating your magnificent life. *Don't look to the left or the right.* Look within, and only be concerned about *your* path and your purpose. You can't have someone else's destiny.

You matter. Your dreams matter. Your destiny is for you only. And, don't let money stop you from pursuing a life of significance; remember, you are an heir to the kingdom of the most high; your riches are there waiting for you to claim them!

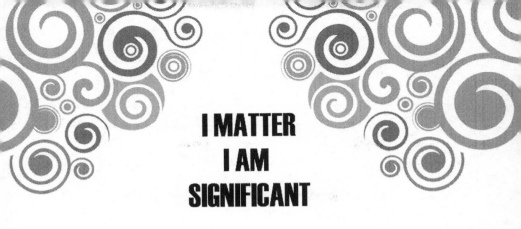

I MATTER
I AM
SIGNIFICANT

How would you describe what MORE looks like for you?

_____
_____
_____
_____

What special gifts do you have?

_____
_____
_____
_____

What kind of relationship do you have with money?

_____
_____
_____
_____

What lessons have you been taught about money?

_____
_____
_____
_____

How can you use your gifts to make money?

_____

_____

_____

_____

What signs do you see that are telling you it's time to make a move and or experience *more* in your life?

_____

_____

_____

_____

What boundaries do you need to put in place so people will respect you and your time?

_____

_____

_____

_____

What do you *believe* you deserve?

_____

_____

_____

_____

What are you going to do to raise your deserve level?

_____

_____

_____

_____

What is missing in your life?

_____

_____

_____

_____

How do you plan to make a difference in the world?

_____

_____

_____

_____

"Silence is the language of God, all else

is poor translation."

— Rumi

CHAPTER 7

Chapter 7
Slow Down to Speed Up Your Significance

ACTIVATE HARMONY

"Living your grandest dream will require you to be your grandest you." – Catrice M. Jackson

We're all chasing and pursuing something. We yearn for that thing or that someone that will make us feel better. Consciously and unconsciously we reach for feelings. We reach for something that will take the pain away, so we grab pain medication, food, participate in sex, excessively sleep, or do whatever will alleviate our pain and suffering. We reach for happiness by indulging in something that makes us feel good: a funny movie, a scoop of our favorite ice cream or spending time with people we love. We reach for hope by praying, meditating, spending time alone or talking to a trusted friend. In every moment of our lives, we reach for *something* or someone to feel or not feel our way through life.

Reaching and searching for *something* to help us feel or *not feel* is *very* normal. I don't know one person who does not navigate through life this way. It's true; some people are better at reaching for healthy options than others, but, nonetheless, we all are seekers. I'm learning how to seek healthier options every day, but there are days when I'm having a valley moment and it takes longer to reach for something healthy; something that will pull me out of the pity pit instead of making the hole deeper. It takes mindfulness, the right choices, and often the *love* of God to remind me that I AM a daughter of the most high; therefore, I deserve the best!

Seeking is how we discover who we are, who others are, what we are here to do and what our ultimate purpose is in life. The seeker's path is sure to include pitfalls, detours, roadblocks, valleys, mountain tops and epiphanies. Seeking is how we make sense out of our lives and our circumstances. If we didn't seek, we'd aimlessly move through the world with no real purpose or destination. Do you feel like this? Does it feel like you're just existing, living day by day with no clear intention, purpose, plan or destination? Remember, *your soul knows the way!* Today, I challenge you to seek in new directions. When you feel the need to reach for a feeling, instead of reaching outside of yourself, I want you to reach *within* yourself.

It's essential I keep reminding you that your soul knows the way, and that your purpose is to love and serve. Ellie Drake, Leader of *Braveheart Women*, once shared with me that we should have a personal, professional and global purpose. I thought this was brilliant, and it really resonated with me. I believe it, and I know what my three purposes are. If your purpose is that you are here to love and serve, shouldn't you begin with you? Let me expand on this. Yes, I also believe I am here to love and serve God, and when I love and serve myself, I am loving and serving the God in me. Maybe you don't believe in God. Maybe you call your higher power something else. Nevertheless, loving and serving you is a beautiful, healthy an honorable choice.

HOW SLOWING DOWN OPENS THE CHANNEL TO HEAR YOUR SOUL SPEAK

Chasing and pursuing! Chasing and pursuing; does that feel overwhelming or exhausting to you? Do you ever get tired of always being mentally and emotionally on the go? I do, and so I pause. Sometimes you've got to pause in order to move forward and slow down to speed up. The most prolific and profound pieces of wisdom come to me in two places: the shower and the kitchen. I'm sure I'm not alone with the belief that the best ideas and inspiration drop into my spirit when I'm taking a shower. How about you? Do you get divine inspiration when you are showering?

There's actually some scientific research that suggests why we get the best ideas and inspiration in the shower. When we are moving, thinking, acting, engaging and busy doing in life, it doesn't give our minds enough time to slow down and fully process all of the brilliance we have within us. Ever notice when you are daydreaming that your mind is a bit more carefree and spontaneous? Aha moments, epiphanies, prophetic visions, creative glimpses, innovative ideas and the *knowing* occur more often and more vividly when our minds are relaxed. The unconscious mind is freed up to play, create, envision and dialogue with you!

According to Washington University Psychologist R. Keith Sawyer, and author of the new book *Explaining Creativity: The Science of Human Innovation*, says when these magical mental moments occur, the mind is unoccupied with busy work and is able to play a splendid game of free association. Free association is when the mind wanders and connects unassociated thoughts with other unassociated thoughts and connect the dots so to speak. During this glorious game, the command center (the place where decisions and goals are activated) shuts down and play time ensues. When you're in the shower, you relax, your brain relaxes and creative juices are activated through the wonder of wandering.

I often receive insight, experience aha moments and get innovative and creative ideas when I'm cooking. I love to cook. It truly is a creative form of artistry for me. I sometimes cook what I call pantry meals, meaning there is no plan or recipe. I look in the cabinets and the refrigerator and one ingredient becomes the culinary catalyst for a scrumptious creation. It could be me spotting the jar of pesto in the refrigerator, and then thinking, what goes well with pesto? The ideas pour in, and intuitively, the next ingredient comes to mind, and then before you know it, I've created something unexpectedly delicious. While all of this mixing, tasting, stirring, and creating takes place, re-occurring questions are answered, problems are solved and ideas are born. I absolutely love it!

You have no idea how many shower breaks or cooking pauses I've taken while writing this book (smile). Did you know when you're relaxed in the shower, you release a neurotransmitter (brain chemicals that communicate information) called *Dopamine*? Yes, it's known as the *happy-go-lucky* chemical within the brain. Any who, I digressed a bit. However, relaxing, slowing down, and pausing, allows your mind to uncover answers to your burning questions. The delight of daydreaming fosters in fresh ideas and ignites creative sparks. When you unwrap the gift of doing nothing, you tune in to the station of your soul, and it speaks in a language we call hunches, intuition and what I refer to as the *knowing*.

I'll admit, slowing down is a challenge for me. I'm naturally driven and intrinsically motivated. I have BIG dreams. I know my purpose. Creative ideas come easily to me, and my brain's command center seems to be ready to rock at all times. I love this quote, "*some people wake up to alarm clocks; others to a calling* (unknown author)." It's true! Which one are you waking up to? Do you wake up to the dread of another day or do you wake up with expectation that something wonderful will either happen or you'll create it?

Not long after my eyes open, and shortly after I give thanks for another day to live, learn, love and serve, ideas begin to flood in. One of my new favorite questions to ask myself in the morning is, "what's possible?" The flood gates open and idea after idea rushes into my spirit. *What can I create today? Who can I serve today? How can I be more significant in the world? What do I need and want to do today to live my dream at a greater capacity?* And yes, the occasional "*oh my gosh, how am I going to get it all done in this lifetime,*" question pops into my head. The questions, answers, ideas and my divine assignment cause me to leap out of bed every morning. Well, let me clarify; my body doesn't always leap, but my mind does.

Stop! My body screams. *No, let's play, let's create, let's work*, says my mind. Maybe it's the soon to be Psychologist in me that my brain is in steady motion. I've learned to pause. I've learned to stop, and I'm still learning. Do you feel like there is too much to do? Do you feel like you don't have enough time for yourself? Do you desire to give more attention to dreams, hopes, desires and plans? Have you heard this saying before, "*everyone gets the same 24 hours in a day; it's up to you how you use them.*" Well, this is true, and so how do others accomplish their goals and manifest their dreams and others do not?

Many would suggest we create work-life balance. I don't believe in work-life balance; instead, I believe in creating harmony. One definition of harmony is *a consistent, orderly or pleasing arrangement of parts; congruity*. I like this idea better. Balance suggests perfecting a position where parts (of your life) are equal, whereas harmony suggests creating consistent order that brings peace, pleasure, and alignment. Have you been trying to balance it all? What if, instead, you worked to create and allow harmony into your life? Here's how you can begin.

THREE PILLARS OF INNER PEACE: Creating Harmony

CONSISTENCY: Means adherence to the same principles over time. What routines do you engage in every day? What principles have you set for how you live? If you follow your routines and principles every day, you will receive the results they are designed to produce. If you eat healthy and exercise for thirty minutes every day, your *routine* should yield the *result* of better health and weight loss. Conversely, if you don't exercise and eat junk food, you will not feel healthy or lose weight. The key to consistency is to make sure you not only practice your routine the same way every time but that the routine itself is "right for you." If you want more peace and harmony in life, look at your routine. What practices and principles do you need to change or add into your daily life? First, identify the results you want to see in your life, and then find the *right* routine for you to get what you want. If you change the routine, your results will change!

ORDER: Means in a state of proper arrangement, preparation or readiness. Where there is clutter, there is chaos. Where there is uncleanliness, there is chaos. Where there is lack of order, there is stagnation and the inability to experience clarity and progression. Clutter, uncleanliness and chaos are the breeding ground for settling, mediocrity and living a life less than what you deserve. What is out of order in your life? Where are things and situations unclean? Look around your home, car, office or living space;

is it dirty, cluttered or unsanitary? How can you expect to experience clarity, harmony and progression if your living space is cluttered and stagnant? Clean up your spaces! Cleaning up your external spaces will help clean up your internal spaces: your mind, heart and soul. Have you heard the famous idiom, "*cleanliness is next to godliness*?" Those words are not exactly written in the Holy Scripture; however, the scriptures are full of messages about the importance of "being/living" clean. Even if you don't believe in God or prescribe to the teachings of the *Word of God*, clean up your spaces! You will instantly feel lighter, more focused, clearer and maybe even inspired to move forward!

CONGRUITY: *Means being in alignment and experiencing harmony.* When your thoughts, feelings and actions line up to produce the results you desire, you are *being* congruent. If you say you want peace, but start arguments with everyone, you are not congruent. When you say you want to lose weight but don't eat healthy and exercise, you are being incongruent. When you say you want a better life but don't take action to change your life, you are being incongruent. When you are incongruent in your thoughts, behaviors and actions there is *dis-ease* in your life. The dis-ease of apathy, the dis-ease of settling, the dis-ease of bitterness and dis-ease after dis-ease! Where there is dis-ease, there is no peace, pleasure or harmony. You know what disease does to your body; dis-ease does the same thing. Dis-ease ravages your mind and spirit and destroys your dreams.

Instead of trying to create work-life balance, strive for creating harmony in your home and in your life. Strive towards creating harmony within your relationships. Get your physical and mental house in order. Create and implement healthy routines for your mind, body and spirit. Think, feel and behave congruently. If you say you're going to do something for yourself and others, be in integrity and do it. Being congruent and cultivating harmony is love in motion. You deserve it, so be loving towards yourself.

Creating harmony in your life is an act of self-love. You deserve harmony and peace. Without them, it will be difficult for you to re-discover your greatness, because, in order for you to hear the voice of your soul, you need to be at peace within, and your external environment needs to be free from chaos. Love yourself enough to clean up! Love yourself enough to put things in order. Love yourself enough to be consistent in your thoughts, feelings and behaviors. Nobody wants to be around, help or support people who are moody and emotionally all over the place. Love yourself enough to make promises to yourself and keep them. You are worthy of all of this luscious love and more.

SELF-LOVE AND PERSONAL PURPOSE

If you recall, I stated earlier that your purpose simplified is you are here to love and serve. You cannot truly love others if you don't love yourself. It is difficult to be of great service to others when you don't know how to be of great service to yourself. When things have a purpose in your life, they matter, they are meaningful and you know the value of their existence. *You are no different.* You matter, and your life has meaning! You have purpose simply by existing. The first step to deeply discovering your bigger purpose and unleashing your significance is to identify, clarify and honor your own *personal* purpose.

Your personal purpose is *just for you*. You are the focal point. Your personal purpose is to love and serve yourself so you can be of great service to the world. It's been said that *you cannot serve from an empty cup,* and I believe that to be true. If your mind is cluttered and confused, your heart is broken and bruised, and your spirit shattered and miserable, imagine what you would pour out of your cup into the souls of others. And what you pour out may not always be intentional, yet the residue of toxicity of the soul still has a foul smell. I know you desire to give your BEST to the world and serve from a healthy cup, and here's how you begin.

It is time for you to stop... stop the running, chasing, and searching outside of yourself. You don't need permission to be you. You don't need approval or validation from anyone. You are in total control of your life, and it's up to you to make the BEST choices for you. My *personal purpose* is to be one hundred percent authentically me and speak and live my truth. That is what I choose to do for me, and, if other people don't like it, that's their problem. I don't concern myself with what others think. I *must* be authentic, free to be me and walk in *my* truth. Every day I wake up, that is the promise I live out for me. I'm intentional about sticking to this promise no matter what.

By being authentic, free and living my truth, I am choosing to love and serve ME! So what will your personal purpose be? How will you choose to *love and serve* yourself? What is the ONE promise you will make and keep no matter what? This is where you begin, especially if you do not yet know your bigger purpose or divine assignment. The intent of declaring and living your personal purpose is so you can take care of you, show love and dedication to yourself, and begin creating harmony from the inside out.

One of the most important steps of defining your personal purpose is to identify what values are important to you. I encourage my clients to identify and live by 5 core values personally and professionally. Personal values powerfully serve as a guide post, a blue print and a daily reminder of who you are and what's important to you. Many people aimlessly go through life, and then wonder why life is not pleasurable and peaceful. You got to wake up every day with intention, and go about your day with focus and purpose if you want it to be rich and meaningful.

What values are important to you? Think about it. If you had to live your life by only five values, what would they be? Think of these values as a container for your calling. The values should reflect the *truest* part of your soul. Who are you when no one is around? Who are you when you strip down naked? What is important to you? How do you want to show up for yourself? Review the partial list of values and determine which values speak to you. Decide which 5 values you want to use as your guide post, blue print and daily reminder for who you want to be, how you want to live, and how you want love, and show up for yourself. If you don't see a value on the list, add it.

Core Value List

Love	Family	Adventure
Joy	Peace	Integrity
Inner Peace	Intimacy	Intelligence
Honesty	Passion	Motivation
Achievement	Comfort	Beauty
Creativity	Courage	Travel
Success	Spirituality	Respect
Leadership	Learning	Faith
Independence	Belonging	Purpose
Happiness	Relaxation	Confidence
Abundance	Fame	Serenity
Grace	Healing	Recognition
Faith	Wisdom	Excitement
Exploration	Inspiration	Empowerment
Nature	Diversity	Simplicity
Harmony	Freedom	Health
Play	Reliability	Patience
Curiosity	Charity	Service
Friendship	Excellence	Prosperity

What five values did you choose? Make sure you chose values that speak to who you want to be and not what other people expect you to be.

The values should be true to who you already are. For example, my top five core values are *Authenticity, Truth, Freedom, Peace* and *Inspiration,* and here's why. I've always been authentic, and it's my number one core value because if I can't be me, I don't want to exist. I need and love the truth. I seek and speak the truth and want others to be truthful with me. I need to be free and thrive when I'm free! My soul needs peace. I need peace in my mind, body and spirit, and, when I am in peace instead of pieces, I am clear, creative and focused. Inspiration (being in spirit) is my source of divine connections. I love to be inspired and find immense joy in inspiring others.

Of course there are other values that are important to me, but I could live by these five values alone if I had to and I do. They provide me not only a blueprint for how I choose to be, but also how I choose to live in every space I occupy. My values remind me I can be me without permission or approval, say what I feel without shuddering or shame, move through the world unbothered by what people think and say, be at peace with who I am and how I live, and to always be in spirit with the Divine One. This is what my personal purpose looks like in action!

I want you to spend some time in deep thought about how you want to and choose to be, live and occupy space in the world. Do this for you! Create a personal blue print or *code of being* for how you will love and serve yourself. Choose values that will serve your personal desires and needs. Write them down, and remember them always. Then take action and show up as your core values in every moment. Doing so will allow you to begin achieving the congruency and harmony within necessary to begin or amplify your evolving greatness!

"Your relationship with yourself sets the tone for every other relationship you have."– Robert Holden

I love this quote by Oprah Winfrey. *"Nobody but you is responsible for your life. It doesn't matter what your mama did; it doesn't matter what your daddy didn't do. You are responsible for your life. You are responsible for the energy that you create for yourself, and you're responsible for the energy that you bring to others."* THIS IS SO VERY TRUE: I often hear way too many people blaming their parents for the life they are living now. Too many people use the excuses of "*my mom or dad is that way or my mom or dad did this or that to me*" as a justification for *how* they show up in the world. This type of language is a cop-out! When you do this, you fail to take responsibility for the CHOICES you've made and put yourself in the VICTIM BOX. Sure, your parents may have made mistakes and even hurt you, but YOU can always *choose* a new way of being.

ENERGY IS SO IMPORTANT: Silent energy and direct energy are both powerful. Have you ever had "someone" come around, not say a word and just suck the life out of you? Do you know people who just seem to *never* be happy? That energy is unattractive! If you carry that kind of energy, you NOT only repel people you love or want to attract, but you repel blessings, opportunities, open doors, answered prayers and anything else you REALLY want. Your energy is like a magnet. If it's negative, you attract negative; if it's positive, you attract positive. How can you take FULL RESPONSIBILITY FOR YOUR LIFE NOW? What will you do to transform your energy from negative to positive to attract what you desire?

Change what you chase! Yearn for something deep within YOU! Consciously reach within and identify what you're feeling. Is it a love or fear feeling? Acknowledge it and choose as often as you can to BE love. It's not always easy, but it is possible and necessary. Every time you choose love over fear, you win and those around you win, too. Choosing to be love, to love you and love others is the healthy choice. You, your mind, body and soul deserves that. Give it to yourself because you matter, you are magnificent, you are significant!

Slow down. Now is all you have. You can activate your purpose by first defining what your personal purpose is. Who do you want to be for you? Define it. How do you want to love and serve yourself? Define it. This is one time you get to be selfish. What kind of energy do you want to exude and sprinkle into the lives of others? Define it. Don't be distracted by how other people show up in the world or what they are doing on their destiny path. This is the perfect opportunity for you to define HOW you will live out YOUR destiny dash and play by your own rules. The possibilities are limitless! The world is waiting for the REAL you to show up and shine. Make sure you do it like the star you already are!

> "God's definition of what matters is pretty straightforward. He measures our lives by how we love." — Francis Chan

I MATTER
I AM
SIGNIFICANT

What have you been chasing in life?

_____

_____

_____

_____

What have you been searching for?

_____

_____

_____

_____

What is your personal purpose?

_____

_____

_____

_____

When do you get your best ideas or have moments of inspiration?

_____

_____

_____

_____

What do you do to slow down?

_____
_____
_____
_____

What would ideal inner peace feel like for you?

_____
_____
_____
_____

In what ways is your life out of order?

_____
_____
_____
_____

How will you create harmony in your life?

_____
_____
_____
_____

What kind of _dis-ease_ are you experiencing?

_____
_____
_____
_____

How would you describe your current status of self-love?

_____
_____
_____
_____

What do you really value?

_____
_____
_____
_____

Describe the energy you bring with you?

_____
_____
_____
_____

What kind of energy do you want to bring with you?

_____
_____
_____
_____

How will you begin to love you better?

_____
_____
_____
_____

"When people can't handle your light,

don't take it personal and don't shrink.

Either they will choose to shine or put on

a pair of shades."

— Catrice M. Jackson

CHAPTER 8

Chapter 8
The Audacity to Be You

ACTIVATE AUDACITY

"Don't ask yourself what the world needs. Ask yourself what makes you come alive and then go do that. Because what the world needs is people who have come alive." – Howard Thurman

Imagine waking up in a new, strange but familiar place; a city that you've never been to before. You stagger to the window not yet fully awake. The sun is shining brightly from its highest position in the ocean blue sky. You look out the window and see friendly faces that ooze with joy, delight and excitement. Everyone seems to be happy and in great spirits. People are dancing in the streets and skipping happily down the sidewalks and greeting others along the way. You wonder where you are; the vibe feels electric and intriguing! Curiously, you go outside to see *why* everyone is so delighted to be alive.

You begin to converse with strangers who oddly seem like family. One woman obviously high on life says, *"Welcome home; we're thrilled you decided to come back!"* Home, you think, knowing full well *this* is not *your* home. Everyone you meet is happily shining their light and illuminating the world with contagious gratitude and cheer. You stop in the coffee shop to get your favorite wake me up beverage, and the barista bubbles with joy and serves you with deep gladness.

Conversation after conversation you realize everyone simply feels alive inside. It's not a holiday or a special occasion; it's a regular day in the lives of *ordinary* people. These are ordinary people who have *chosen* to *be significant* and live extraordinary lives; lives that make them feel ignited inside. You just encountered a neighborhood full of people who have found the *value* in living. They are living a life they love, and it's undeniable! They are serving others with love and grace. These ordinary people have chosen to be happy and helpful and to do it with extraordinary meaning. They've *chosen* to *be* GREAT!

Today's the day *you* choose to be significant and GREAT! Greatness is not only for the elite, rich and famous. Significance is not reserved for a select few. There are endless stories of people with numerous odds stacked against them who *chose* to rise above their circumstances and triumph for you to *not* believe it's possible for you to do the same. Maybe you know the story of Chris Gardner, who struggled with homelessness while raising his son and working as a stockbroker. Chris was relentless in making his dreams a reality, and he did by never giving up and starting his own brokerage firm, later to sell it for multi-millions. He went on to write his autobiography "*The Pursuit of Happiness,*" which was later turned into a blockbuster movie.

According to the odds stacked against him, he would have been expected to not "amount to anything" in life, but Chris Gardner refused to accept mediocrity as his destiny, and instead *chose* to unleash his significance and be great in the world. J.K Rowling is another great example of choosing greatness despite her circumstances. J.K. Rowling, the author of the world renowned book series, *Harry Potter*, was once homeless, living off of public assistance and a single mother who refused to give up. Her first novel, *Harry Potter and The Philosopher's Stone* was rejected by several leading publishers. She did not quit! Once this book became published, she became known as one of the world's best paid modern writers and is one of the first billionaire writers.

Chris Gardner and J.K. Rowling believed in their gift and greatness even when there was no external evidence to justify their belief in something invisible to the human eye. One truth we can extract from their stories is they *knew* what made them feel *alive* inside. They had a deep *knowing* there was *something* (unexplainable to others) they were meant to be, do and share with the world. And, I imagine they were perceived to be "crazy" for believing in a vision that others could not see and trusting that their soul knew the way. Their stories may appear to be unique because they are famous, yet there are everyday ordinary people like you who have overcome horrendous life challenges to answer the call in their soul to live extraordinary lives. Their call does not and will not look like *your* call. You may not create a famous rags to riches story. You may never write a New York Times best-selling book or close a multi-million dollar business deal, and you don't have to in order to unleash your significance. You can be GREAT at whatever your soul is begging you to do!

Your greatness is not elusive. It's not hiding or running from you. In fact, your greatness is standing still waiting for you to chase it, tackle it down and say "yes" to it. It's always been chasing you; you've just been occupied with life and the challenges it brings. It's there! *Your purpose, your calling, your magnificence is waiting to be unleashed!*

Any one walking in their greatness chose to BE great. In order to fully walk in your greatness you too have to *choose* to BE all you are destined to be. So many people get it wrong. They believe once they do something great and accumulate certain material things then they can be all they are destined to be. That is so far from the truth. The truth is you must first BE, then DO and then HAVE what you desire. Have you been wondering why you have yet to manifest or actualize your dreams and the lifestyle you desire? Maybe you've got it wrong too.

Here's a perfect example of how someone has it *wrong* (out of order). When an ordinary person wins a million-dollar lottery payout and within a year they are broke, the having and doing happened before the being. In other words, they used the money to *do* and *have* millionaire things. They didn't spend (save or invest) the money *wisely* and failed to develop millionaire thoughts and beliefs from the inside out to sustain their millionaire status. Are you working towards your greatness out of order? Are you giving more energy to doing things and being busy and obtaining material things to look like a millionaire, to *appear to be* walking in your greatness? T. Harv Eker, author of *Secrets of the Millionaire Mind* says that you must master the inner game of wealth before you can BECOME wealthy and sustain it. It's true, just like the caterpillar BECOMES a butterfly from the inside out before the world sees its magnificence and it takes flight! Greatness is always an inside job.

> *"We delight in the beauty of the butterfly, but rarely admit the changes it has gone through to achieve that beauty." -Maya Angelou*

Being... is the first step towards unleashing your significance and walking in your greatness. Keep this simple formula in mind, **BE + DO + HAVE = living a significant life**. So many people searching for significance in life ask the question *what do I want to do* before asking the question *who do I want to become*? We've been conditioned to go, go, go and do, do, do, but we were never properly taught how to *be* authentically who we already are and to evolve into our highest selves (the best version of you). Let's start with how to BE the best version of you!

Who do you want to *be* until you take your last breath? I'm not talking about what you want to have, experience or accomplish. I'm talking about when you sit in the dark all by yourself with no distractions behind the curtain of the stage of life. The *being* I speak of does not include any titles, degrees, certifications, income, possessions or your career. The being I speak of doesn't include anyone else; it's just *you in solitude* with your intimate thoughts and feelings. Who you are behind the curtain is the prelude to your on stage performance (how you show up in the world). You better believe that every superstar before they take the stage BELIEVES they are about to kill it! They know what their gift is, who they are, and they deliciously serve it to us, and we love it.

How do you want to deliciously serve YOU to the world? Think about who you were (thoughts, behaviors and actions) just a year ago; are you a better person from the inside out? What have you learned? How have you transformed? Hopefully you've become wiser, kinder, more compassionate and better at navigating your way through your life. Hopefully your relationships have improved, and you've become more insightful, intuitive and brave. If so, how did you accomplish this? What did you do? I suspect you learned from experiences, made different choices, thought different thoughts and behaved in new ways. That's exactly what you *must* do to evolve into the next level of the best version of you. With every new level, you'll be required to up level your thoughts and actions. *Here are 8 actions you can take now to level up!*

HOW TO BECOME THE BEST VERSION OF YOU

HONOR WHO YOU ARE RIGHT NOW:

Comparing yourself to others sucks the life out of who you are. The only one you should compete with daily is yourself. Strive to be a better you every second of the day. You are not the same person you were a year ago, and you'll be a different person a year from now, but, only if you honor who you are right now in *this* very moment. You're still here, you made it, and you survived experiences you didn't think you would. Be proud of the steps you've taken and the things you've accomplished. Someone you know wishes they were you and could have what you have. Give thanks for everything! Be grateful for who you are, what you have, and how far you've traveled in your journey. Sure, you've got work to do and changes to make in your life, but stop for a second and account for and HONOR all the goodness and greatness you already possess. You matter. **You have value. You are worthy. You are significant**. How will you honor you as you are right now?

START A NEW LOVING RELATIONSHIP WITH YOURSELF:

Love is the most powerful energy source that exists. If you are not loving on you and loving you right now, you cannot expect others to love on you and honor your value. I agree with Dr. Phil McGraw who says, "*We teach people how to treat us.*" The way you love and care for yourself is the blueprint by which others will use to treat you. If people are not treating your "right," check yourself. In what ways are you not treating you right? What behaviors are giving other people the *permission* to mistreat you? Change the way you view yourself. Shift the way you speak about yourself. Choose to love you better than anyone else ever could. I love what Rudy Francisco says, "*perhaps we should love ourselves so fiercely, that when others see us they know exactly how it should be done.*" What does loving yourself fiercely look like? I want you to make a list of the 10 behaviors you desire others to treat you with fierce love and then start treating yourself that way: intentionally, repeatedly, and consistently. Love and all its glorious versions are highly attractive. Love you, be love, think and act lovingly, and what you love will be attracted to you. **You matter. You have value. You are worthy. You are significant**. How will you love you as you are right now?

CHOOSE TO RE-DISCOVER YOURSELF:

It's so easy to lose yourself in the pursuit of success, while striving towards your goals, when you're in relationships and on the day to day walk of life. Have you forgotten what makes you smile? Did you tuck away special talents the world says are not useful? Have you let dreams that were once on fire fizzle out? I believe that God doesn't make mistakes! If you have special talent, skills and abilities that come naturally for you, are you using them? It's time to embark on a journey of self discovery! What brings you joy and peace? What or who makes you laugh? What excites you? What makes you feel good inside? What talent or skills would you love to revive? What makes you happy? Dig deep, find it, bring it to the surface, do it more often and be with people who encourage you to be you, and do you. Don't let the world eat you alive, and don't serve yourself up on a silver platter to be devoured. Audre Lorde says it best, *if I didn't define myself for myself, I would be crunched into other people's fantasies for me and eaten alive.*" FIND YOU AGAIN! **You matter. You have value. You are worthy. You are significant**. How will you begin to re-discover you?

FOLLOW YOUR BLISS:

Joseph Campbell says, "*Follow your bliss. Find it where it is, and don't be afraid to follow it.*" On the journey to unleash your significance, you often stray far away from home. You get lost in the woods like Hansel and Gretel. You end up in the *Land of Oz* on the yellow brick road desperately trying to find your way home. You must be like Dorothy from the Wizard of Oz and remember *there is no place like home*. Home is your heart and soul. What and who you love the most already lives there. Your bliss lives there. Your bliss is that which ignites, insights, inspires, intrigues, and delights you. Your bliss is the place where passion, peace, joy, beauty, wonder, creativity and curiosity lives. It's your soul's sweet spot! The way you find your way back home to follow your bliss is to pay attention to the bread crumbs of life. When Hansel and Gretel ventured off into the woods, they left a trail of bread crumbs so they could find their way back home. If you pay close attention and tune in to your life (stop focusing on other people's lives), you will see and hear the bread crumbs (hints, nudges, whispers, clues and calls) in your own life. They're there. They've always been there, but you've been too busy trying to figure out how to get ahead or how to survive that you have missed them. Open your mind and soul to following your bliss, do it afraid, and let it lead you back home to the place where your soul knows. **You matter. You have value. You are worthy. You are significant**. How will you begin to follow your bliss today?

CHANGE AND EXPAND YOUR CIRCLE OF FRIENDS:

The people you hang out with, engage with, spend time with, and are in relationship with and those who you give your time have a huge impact on who you will become and the direction in which you'll go in life. You shouldn't have to think long and hard about who the *right* people are for you. Just feel them! ENERGY IS EVERYTHING. We all have an aura, an invisible tone and a vibrational energy that comes with us and lingers after we have left the room. Think about the six people you spend the most time with. Write their names on a piece of paper, and then list words or phrases that describe how you FEEL when you are with them. They will either invoke love feelings or fear feelings. Since no one is perfect, they are sure to invoke both types of feelings. The key is to determine whether someone invokes more love feelings than fear feelings. If being in the company of someone makes you feel inadequate, uncertain, anxious, doubtful, scared, timid or angry, *these people are toxic to your soul*. If it doesn't FEEL right to be with them, it isn't right to be with them. Take serious note, and begin to remove them from your life or decrease the amount of time you spend with them. Your soul not only knows the way; it knows *who* to take on the journey with you. Choose people to be in your life that invoke LOVE feelings. These are people who love you, support, encourage and celebrate you, challenge you to be better and push you to raise your standards. Choose people who got your back, people who make you smile and those who are genuinely happy for you. You DESERVE a fabulous circle of friends; go find them! **You matter. You have value. You are worthy. You are significant.** How will you begin to change or expand your circle of friends today?

RAISE YOUR EMOTIONAL INTELLIGENCE LEVEL:

It's been said that your *Intelligence Quotient* or your IQ (what you know based on standardized testing) will get you the job, but it's your *Emotional Intelligence* or EI (also known as EQ) that will help you keep the job or get the promotion. In other words, who you are and how you behave is what will attract and sustain the job, career, relationships, clients and opportunities you desire. Emotional Intelligence is the ability and capacity to recognize your own and other people's emotions and feelings and to use them to calculate your thoughts, feelings or behaviors.

Here's a great example. You've had a horrible day, and your friend texts you to ask if she can come over to talk about a problem she is having. Upon arriving, she begins to tell you her problem; she's visually distraught and feeling pretty bad about the situation. You notice and then proceed to tell her how horrible *your* day was. Before you know it, your friend is consoling you, and the focus is now about you and *your* problem. Your friend leaves feeling ignored, and her situation is unresolved. You text your friend hours later and get no response. In this case, you lacked the ability to properly respond to the emotional cues of your friend and failed to provide the emotional support she needed. If this were a real situation, you lacked Emotional Intelligence in this case.

How many times have you pretended to listen to someone but instead were planning your response? How many times do you ignore the emotional cues of others? How often do you allow your emotions to consume you, take over and sabotage your relationships? Nobody wants to be around people who are emotionally ignorant, self-serving, lacking compassion, easily irritated, and or clueless to emotional cues. If you want to keep or be promoted in your job, raise your EI. If you desire to attract and sustain healthy, loving relationships, raise your EI. If you want to get more clients and referrals, raise your EI. The higher your EI the greater your positive vibrational energy will be. Energy is everything! BE what you want to attract. **You matter. You have value. You are worthy. You are significant**. How will you begin to elevate your Emotional Intelligence?

BECOME UNBOTHERED AND UNMOVED:

How much time and energy are you wasting worrying about what other people are doing, saying and thinking? If you really knew how much they are NOT thinking about you, you'd stop letting it stress you out. Most people are far too egocentric to be that deeply concerned with you. Most people care *more* about what they are doing and what they are experiencing in life. Time is your most precious and valuable resource. Jackie Dorman confirms this by saying *"Anything that costs you your peace is too expensive."* Excusez Moi! Tell your ego to go sit down and shut up! Quit being bothered and moved by the thoughts, opinions and actions of others. When you allow what "they will say or think" to hinder your progress or paralyze your purpose pace, you are focusing on the wrong problems. I whole heartedly agree with TD Jakes when he says *"the only problems you should be concerned about are the ones blocking the path of your purpose."* Booyah! That is the hot naked truth!

Unleashing your significance and walking in your greatness requires you to be unbothered by the naysayers and unmoved by the actions of others. You need to become obsessively focused on you, loving you, releasing your gifts, walking in your purpose, becoming the best version of you and serving the world. Your destiny doesn't have time for dead ends, doubt, Debbie

Downers, distractions, detours and the opinions of others. Stop wasting your most valuable resource of time on the wrong people and situations. BE unbothered. BE unmoved. **You matter. You have value. You are worthy. You are significant**. How will you begin to become unbothered and unmoved?

PRACTICE RADICAL BELIEF AND BE INTENTIONAL:

So far I've shared many powerful points to catapult you into your destiny such as *Clarity is King, Energy is Everything, Love is The Most Powerful Source*, and *You Have Greatness Within You*, and many others. Here's another one: *Believing is Magical and Powerful*. Here's the truth. Any and everything I've ever overcame, accomplished or triumphed over was the result of relentless *Radical Belief* in myself and the possibility to make it a reality. Conversely, any and everything I've failed to accomplish or achieve either I didn't deeply believe it was possible or was not committed enough to do the work. It really is that simple, and I'm totally okay with this truth. I accept it and do not blame anyone for my lack of success.

What is radical belief? I define radical belief as extreme, non-traditional, convicted belief. It's fanatical, relentless and obsessive! Have you ever seen video footage of a crowd of fans responding to the late King of Pop Michael Jackson? They are emotionally consumed, obsessively in awe of his greatness; they cry, scream, reach out to touch him, and some literally pass out from celebrity overwhelm. They are extreme, non-traditional, fanatical fans. There is nothing you can say to convince them that he is not the greatest performer ever.

Do you believe in you like this? Are you fanatical about creating your future? Are you obsessed with your dreams, desires and purpose? Any and everything you want to be, do and have will require you to practice daily radical belief. Every single day of your life you've got to believe it before you experience it. Whatever it is for you, if you don't believe, you won't achieve or receive it.

You may have to believe in things you cannot see, and to help you turn the invisible into the tangible, you *must* be intentional. This means your thoughts and actions must be deliberate, willful, calculated, conscious and purposeful all day every day. Your dreams are not going to knock on your door and say, "*here I am.*" You have to intentionally make them happen, and create harmony and alignment from the inside out to move in the flow of graceful manifestation. Stop waking up and letting life happen. Stop allowing others to choose your path. Stop waiting on miracles to fall in your lap. Get up and do something intentional to create the life you desire to live. I promise when you practice radical belief and become intentional, any and everything you desire you *will* be, do and have. **You matter. You have value. You are worthy. You are significant**. How will you start practicing radical belief and purposeful intention today?

> *"A strong spirit transcends rules." – Prince*

AWAKEN THE AUDACITY TO BECOME ALIVE

Over the years and on my personal journey to unleashing my significance and walking in my greatness, I've learned to embrace the power of one forbidden word and all that it means. That word is *audacity*! Every audacious person you know will tell you one thing clearly; audacity takes courage, and, when you exercise it, people may not like it or you. This is a fact. When you begin to say, "*so what*" to what other people think of you and start doing your own thing your own way, it's going to make people uncomfortable. When you stop dimming your light and shine like the star you are, it will make people feel threatened. When you start making moves, walking in your greatness and become visible and unstoppable, it will piss people off. You want to know what I say about that? "*Let the pissing begin!*"

Certainly, I don't suggest you go around pissing people off just for kicks, but you're not here to please others and live a life other people want you to live. If loving you, being you and doing you ticks people off, that is none of your business, and you shouldn't be concerned about it. When you choose to transform your ordinary into extraordinary, *that's audacious*! When you finally discover what makes you feel alive inside and begin to live an undeniable significant life, *that is audacious*! When you choose to use your divine gifts to happily serve the world regardless of what the naysayers say, *that is audacious*! It takes audacity to own and walk in your greatness, and anyone you admire for doing so activated the audacity to do it unapologetically. What makes you come alive?

If you're not sure, here are a few classic signs to help you identify what makes you come alive inside so you can audaciously follow your bliss. It will make you leap out of bed. It will bring you complete satisfaction. It will call your name every day. It will make you feel FULL. It will excite you. It will fulfill you and bring you tremendous joy. Look for the bread crumbs. Pay attention to whispers. Trust nudges from your soul. Look for the bliss. Be your bliss. Just be. *Don't ask for approval. Don't wait for permission. Be audaciously you.* Unleash what makes you come alive and go out into the world and do that with overwhelming audacity! **You matter. You have value. You are worthy. You are significant.**

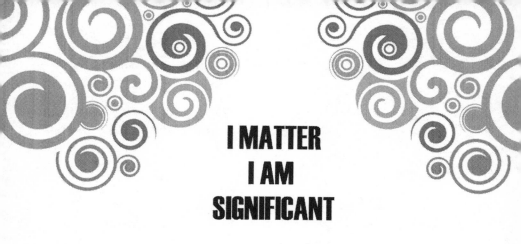

I MATTER
I AM
SIGNIFICANT

What kind of life would you like to wake up to every day?

_____
_____
_____
_____

You have greatness within you, do you know what it is?

_____
_____
_____
_____

What have you overcome that you should celebrate?

_____
_____
_____
_____

What is your big crazy dream?

_____
_____
_____
_____

How can audacity help you live your dream?

_____
_____
_____
_____

Who do you choose to be?

_____
_____
_____
_____

What is your BE+DO+ HAVE formula?

_____
_____
_____
_____

Describe what your best version of you looks and feels like.

_____
_____
_____
_____

What about you can you honor right now?

_____
_____
_____
_____

What do you love about you?

_____

_____

_____

_____

Describe your bliss.

_____

_____

_____

_____

What will you do to follow your bliss?

_____

_____

_____

_____

Who is in your corner?

_____

_____

_____

_____

What type of people do you need to add to your circle?

_____

_____

_____

_____

How has your current level of Emotional Intelligence served you well or hindered you?

_____

_____

_____

_____

What are you willing to practice radical belief for?

_____

_____

_____

_____

What makes you feel alive inside?

_____

_____

_____

_____

"And above all, watch with glittering eyes the whole world around you because the greatest secrets are always hidden in the most unlikely places. Those who don't believe in magic will never find it."

— Roald Dahl

CHAPTER 9

Chapter 9

Create Your Own Magic

ACTIVATE MAGIC

*"Let yourself be drawn by the stronger pull of that which
you truly love." - Rumi*

The world *needs* you and is begging you to show up and do you! What are you waiting for? Do you know how powerfully wonderful and creative you are? Do you realize you can create your own magic or misery? Yes, you are 100% responsible for the moments you experience in your life. Some people are masters at creating magical moments, while others have mastered the game of winning at being miserable. Even in the worst situations, it's up to you to make them meaningful and magical or miserable by choice or default. You already know how to manifest misery because it's so easy to do. *Misery is a magnet* that sucks you in and suffocates the magic in your life, but only if your soul vibration allows it to happen.

Are you a magnet for misery? A miserable moment in your life here or there is to be expected. If you are experiencing "misery" more often than not, here's how you may be vibrating as a misery magnet. Miserable people have a persistent and lingering lack of gratitude. They just can't seem to truly appreciate anything, and it's difficult for them to show even the slightest bit of gratitude. Miserable people are ungrateful and talk more about their burdens than their blessings. Miserable people tend to be bored often and frequently gravitate towards activities laced with drama such as gossiping, watching too much television and hanging out with people who don't really have much going on (other bored or miserable people). It's worth repeating that like attracts like.

Does it look like you are attracting misery so far? Let's look at some more ways you may be attracting misery into your life. Miserable people play on the playground of the past. They are stuck in what used to be, how things were, and often reminisce on the negative experiences that happened to them back in the day. They're still blaming others for the current status of their lives and just can't seem to live in the moment and be grateful for today and all of its goodness. Miserable people's best friend is fear. Fear is their constant companion and follows them around where ever they go. Their best friend has a name, and it's Negative Nelly. Nelly exudes varied characteristics of fear that show up as doubt, worry, anxiety, regret, procrastination, complaining and blame. People usually don't like Nelly, and Nelly doesn't like them.

Miserable people are afraid to take risks, refuse to step outside their comfort zones and often feel stuck yet blame everyone and everything else for their immobility. You'll often find miserable people in the center of or around the edges of drama. They know the latest drama; they love drama filled moments and often are drama queens or kings themselves. Miserable people often have deep trust issues. They question acts of kindness, don't believe what people say and tend to proceed with caution through life if they proceed at all. They think people are out to get them or that others are conspiring against them. When they can't seem to get ahead in life, it's usually someone else's fault.

Miserable people are symptomatic. You'll often hear them express several forms of pain and suffering. Something's always emotionally or physically wrong with them. Something hurts, and they got an ache or a pain here or there. And, they just can't seem to get relief from all of the suffering they are experiencing (cue the woe is me music). With miserable people, if it isn't one thing going on in their life, it's another thing. Complaint, worry, frustration, aggravation, and annoyance after annoyance, nothing seems to bring them joy and rarely do they express deep happiness. Don't you feel exhausted and overwhelmed just reading about all of this misery? It's heavy, draining and dark. Yet, even within this gloomy cloud of existence there *is* a silver lining waiting to shine through for people like this.

Does any of this describe *your* life, your way of being and living? Are you miserable? This is a defining moment to *tell the truth* about the amount of misery you are exuding, attracting and wallowing in. If you lie to yourself, you'll continue to live in the space of settling instead of being all that you are destined to be. Don't allow shame to keep you stuck. One of the most powerful actions I take often is to say *"it is what it is,"* accept it for what it is, and then *choose* to leave it as it is without attachment or make a *new choice* to change my circumstances.

Awareness is the first step in changing anything. If you do NOT acknowledge the problem, the problem will persist. I want you to make a new choice today and change your circumstances. The slightest amount of misery in whatever form it shows up as will cause you to be in the same emotional and spiritual space this time next year. You don't have time for that; you've got great work to do in the world! Any negative or toxic behavior you engage in is the fruit of your thoughts, and, if you want to produce new fruit, you must re-fertilize and transform your roots (your deep subconscious thoughts and beliefs).

You're not a robot! *No one has a remote control to your life but you*! Behavior is not isolated, and *all* behavior occurs for a reason. In my past counseling life, I found it to be extremely helpful to help my clients discover *why* they were feeling and behaving in certain ways, but we did not linger there. I believe the best therapeutic strategies are those where there is intentional focus on accepting *what is* and moving beyond it into something better. I suggest the same to you. Yes, it's important to figure out *why* you may be miserable, unhappy and unfulfilled in your life, but do not linger there! If you do, you'll find yourself spiraling down into the pity pit and feeling worse than before you started searching for the reasons why.

Since it is important to identify why you are stuck, stagnant, paralyzed or procrastinating on unleashing your true significance, let's take a look at a few possible reasons why and what you can do about it. All of these may NOT apply to you, but the key is to take what you need (what's relevant for you) and throw away the rest. The possible causes and new choice list (descriptions/suggestions) is not exhaustive or conclusive. *Please use this information as a guide and not an official or professional diagnosis of any kind.*

Miserable Behavior	Possible Cause	New Choice
Living in the past.	Past emotional wounds that are still oozing with pain. Living in the past is familiar and change is uncomfortable. The past was better and the present moment is too difficult. Unsure of how to move forward. Does not want to deal with current circumstances.	Be grateful for now and what you have in this moment. Choose to forgive those who hurt you and set yourself free. Believe you can create a better today and tomorrow. Tell the truth and choose to live in the present.
Blaming others.	Was blamed as a child/young adult and developed blaming as learned behavior. Taking responsibility is too painful. May feel helpless and blame gives a sense of power. Wants to control others or look like a know it all.	Take responsibility when necessary. Just as you learned this unhealthy behavior, you can choose to unlearn it. Be willing to be vulnerable enough to admit when you're wrong. Practicing vulnerability promotes emotional growth.

Complaining.	Has a sense of entitlement as if the world owes you something. Has extremely high standards and expectations. Tends to have obsessive thoughts of what is concretely right or wrong. May feel inadequate and complaining allows you to feel better than the next person. A learned unhealthy habit.	Accept that no one owes you anything. You are 100% responsible for your thoughts, actions and behaviors. Identify where you feel lack of control in your life and shift the focus on managing your own shortcomings. Show empathy for others and choose healthy ways to honor your greatness instead of pointing the finger at others
Engaging in drama.	May have grown up in a chaotic or drama filled home; therefore, drama feels normal. Drama provides a distraction to dealing with your own unresolved issues. Drama may provide an adrenaline rush that you may be unknowingly addicted to.	Drama is toxic. Step away from it and discover what you're avoiding in your own life. Focus on becoming a better you and protect your spirit from negativity. Practice healthy ways to experience thrill and excitement.

If you've taken the time to examine this chart closely and honestly, you'll clearly see that *misery is a choice*! The choice may be conscious or unconscious, but nevertheless, you are responsible for the presence of or amount of misery in your life. On the other hand, creating meaningful magic in your life is a choice too. When you're miserable, other people around you are miserable, so not only do you have the responsibility to eliminate the misery in your life, you must be responsible for the miserable energy you deposit in the lives of others. *Choosing to stay miserable is self-abuse and projecting your misery onto others is assaultive!* It's an act of violence whether you are giving it (misery) or receiving it from yourself.

Are you ready to stop the pain? Let's do this! I want to show you how to say "no more" to misery and a big "hell yes" to creating meaningful magic in your life. You're going to need a big wand to create all the magic you can stand. Remember..."*Magic is believing in yourself, if you can do that, you can make anything happen (Johann Wolfgang von Goethe).*" What do you want to create? What do you believe you CAN create? I hope your answer is anything! Yes, *anything is possible* to create. What you choose to create may not look like the creations of others, and it is not suppose to. Trying to duplicate someone else's destiny will make you afraid to create your own version of magic.

Creating magic starts with a vision or a dream. This is my seventh published book, and I knew I wanted to create a meaningful, inspirational book that would impact the lives of people from all walks of life. The vision started with one word, *significance.* I wasn't exactly sure what I was going to write about, yet I knew it needed to make a difference in the world. Writing comes naturally to me, but I must admit, the first couple of chapters didn't flow as easily as I expected them to. I had a few moments of frustration and writer's block. I just couldn't seem to find my groove. No matter what, I *believed* I could finish the book and do it with clarity, passion and great purpose. I didn't give up or quit, and here you are about to finish one piece of magic I *believed* I could create!

Being unsure of *what* to create is common. Rumi has the perfect suggestion, he says, "*Respond to every call that excites your spirit.*" Yep, the soul knows! And, guess what? You have what I call *multi-dimensional magic* within you! Inside of you, there is a perfectly imperfect beautiful mosaic of magic *only you* possess. No one in the whole world has the magic recipe you hold in your soul. No one will ever BE you or do your purpose work in the world like you! Do you know *how powerful and special* YOUR magic is? *You are rare and can never be duplicated ever!* That is pure magic all by itself. Can you imagine what your life will be like when you embrace this powerful truth? You are rare pure magic! — So what is magic?

- Magic is turning your words into experiences.
- Magic is moving a dream from distant thought to an intimate reality.
- Magic is making the invisible tangible and touchable.

- Magic is predicting how your life turns out.

- Magic is transforming your physical body and restoring your vitality.

- Magic is purging your soul from everything that paralyzes your purpose.

- Magic is doing work you love and loving the work you do.

- Magic is leaping out of your comfort zone into the unknown and thriving.

- Magic is turning limiting beliefs into limitless possibilities.

- Magic is creating harmony within and living your own unique melody.

- Magic is creating and experiencing moments that take your breath away.

- Magic is trusting your soul knows the way and following it.

- Magic is saying "so what" and living your life unapologetically.

- Magic is slowing down and savoring the silence and synchronicity of life.

- Magic is hearing the whispers of the divine one and saying "yes!"

- Magic is unleashing your gifts and serving the world with them.

- Magic is *not giving a damn* what other people think of you.

- Magic is making a meaningful contribution to humanity.

- Magic is fiercely loving you better than anyone else could ever love you.

- Magic is following your bliss and wallowing in all the goodness and splendor you can imagine.

- Magic is having peace of mind, love in your heart and having a generous spirit.

- Magic is deeply forgiving yourself and choosing to be love and love again.

- Magic is being comfortable in your own skin and appreciating every magnificent part of you.

- Magic is thinking positive thoughts and showing up in the world with optimism.

- Magic is curiosity, creativity and answering the calling for your life.

Magic is unlimited! There are so many ways to create magic in your life your way. Please stop trying to duplicate someone else's life. You'll never live their dreams. You'll never walk their path. You'll never carry out their purpose, and you'll never arrive at their destination. Embrace the awesomeness of your originality, manifest your own dreams, confidently walk your own path and live out your special destiny that's designed just for you!

It's time to create some magic; are you ready? I love to look at creating magic this way. Misery is existing. Mediocrity is surviving, but MAGIC is living and thriving! Dale Carnegie said, *"One of the most tragic things I know about human nature is that all of us tend to put off living. We are all dreaming of some magical rose garden over the horizon – instead of enjoying the roses blooming outside our windows today."* You don't have to look or go far to create magic. You don't need an expensive retreat or any fancy tools or supplies. Magic lives within you and is birthed by your thoughts, beliefs and actions. You can begin creating magic by BELIEVING IN MAGIC and thinking magical thoughts.

Start by declaring who you are and who you want to become. It's been said that the words that follow I AM are what you *will* become. So who do you want to become? Think and declare the highest version of you into existence. Stating I AM declarations is extremely powerful even if you don't fully believe what you state yet. Reprogram and condition your mind into believing what you desire to be or have. You may be broke right now, but you are not poor. Being broke is a temporary situation, whereas *being poor is a state of mind.* So, for example if you want to eliminate your poverty mindset, you must declare I AM WEALTHY. Whatever you want to be or transform declare it with an I AM statement. I want you create five *state of being* I AM declarations right now. You can create as many as you want but create five that you will declare every day until you see what you speak!

I AM_____

I AM_____

I AM_____

I AM_____

I AM_____

According to Proverbs 18:21 (NIV) – *"The tongue has the power of life and death, and those who love it, will eat its fruit."* In other words, if you *speak life*, you'll experience (eat) the consequences of declaring abundance, joy and success. If you speak death (negativity, doom and gloom), you'll experience (eat) the consequences of doubt and disbelief. And to clarify and expand on this, whatever words you speak, that is what you *will* experience. **Declare the magic you want to experience!** Open up your mouth and speak into existence the magical life you desire to live. And then, BELIEVE IT IS HAPPENING NOW.

If you want to be joyful, speak about (talk about) the joy you are experiencing now and want to experience. If you want to be wealthy, express gratitude for the wealth you already have and will have. If you want to experience more love, speak loving thoughts to yourself and others. *Whatever you speak about, you bring about.* Think about what you want. Talk about what you want. Believe you'll have what you want. Expect to receive what you want. Do your part to actualize what you want and what you want will eventually show up like you want. It may not show up *exactly* how you want it to, but it *will* be manifested. BELIEVE in your multi-dimensional magic! Believe. Believe. Believe!

"Respond to every call that excites your spirit."–Rumi

WHAT DO YOU WANT TO DO EVERYDAY FOR THE REST OF YOUR LIFE?

This question seems to trip most people up. Why? Because most people believe they have to work harder than they really need or want to, and we've been conditioned to believe that's true. Don't get me wrong; anything worth having requires hard work and some sacrifice. I want you to consider new possibilities today. What if your work could be magical and meaningful? What if you had the power to infuse some magic into your purpose? What if your magic wand of belief could help you create work you absolutely love? Would you create it?

I used to be a seeker of financial security. I worried about having enough, saving enough and earning enough. Yes, of course, I still desire financial security, but the way I think about what security means now is much different as is the way I *create* money. Some people say money isn't everything, and, to a point, I agree. We need money to live our desired lifestyle and to make the contributions to the world we want to. I've learned how to love money, believe I deserve money, see money as a tool for service, ask for money and use money to create the life I choose to live.

You CAN do work that you love, make the money you desire and be prosperous in a variety of ways. Let's put money to the side for a minute and talk about what you are here to do. WHAT DO YOU WANT TO DO EVERYDAY FOR THE REST OF YOUR LIFE? How do you want to be of service to the world? How do you want to use your gifts to create magic, meaning and make a difference in the lives of others? I understand this can be a difficult question for you, and maybe you've already been seeking the answer.

When I was seeking the answer years ago, I was presented with some great questions to ask myself, and maybe they will help you too. One thing I learned is the *answer* is not always found in the answers themselves, but uncovered in asking the *right* questions. Take out a sheet of paper or your journal and honestly answer these questions. Don't rush it; pause for a moment and listen for the whispers, nudges and answers that come from your heart and soul. Don't force an answer; if one doesn't naturally drop in your spirit, move on to the next one. Just allow the answers to come through to you.

A FEW QUESTIONS TO UNLOCK THE ANSWER TO WHAT AM I HERE TO DO

- If you had unlimited money, what would you do to occupy your time?
- What kind of work do you love so much you would do it for free?
- What skills or talents come natural to you?
- What skills or talent do people consistently compliment you on?
- What skills or talent do you get frequent requests for?
- What legacy do you want to leave behind?
- What activities make you lose track of time?
- If you had to teach something, what would you teach?
- What would you regret not doing if you were to die today?
- What will people say about you at your funeral?
- If you were to start a charity, who would it be for?
- What activities make you feel joyful?
- What was your BIG dream as a child (teen/young adult)?
- Who is doing work that you love and inspires you?
- What social problem would you love to see come to an end?
- What would you jump out of bed every day to do?

Now that you've allowed the answers to come through, look for themes. Pay attention to the questions where answers came quickly and easily. Look for words or phrases that are similar. Notice how you *feel* when you see the answers on paper. What do you see? What is most attractive? What *feels good* and makes your soul tingle? What excites or inspires you? What answers make your soul say YES! YES! YES! Connect the dots and look for that which is not so visible to the eye but crystal clear to your soul. I promise you the answers are there. Keep asking questions, be curious and let your *bliss* drop the bread crumbs to lead you home to your calling. Your soul knows...

Discovering your true calling can take some time and even longer if you just wait for it to knock on your door. Oh, how I love Rumi, thirteenth century Persian poet, and seeker of truth and love! This is one of my favorite quotes of his, "*What you seek is seeking you.*" When I heard this for the first time, my soul cried out yes, yes, yes! What he says is profoundly true. While you are chasing what you seek, it is seeking you. Sometimes you've got to just stop, pause, be still and open up your arms and say, "here I AM!" Your dream, purpose and destiny is NOT running or hiding from you. It's there waiting for you to say, "yes" to it!

As I have said "yes" to my significance I no longer hunger for the traditional, dogmatic definition of success. I'm not thirsty for attention, validation or fame. I can easily move about in the world as if I am the only one in it. I crave being in the company of people who feed my soul with conversations about everything bigger than us. I want to sit at the table with visionaries, scholars, teachers, seekers, healers, rebels and revolutionaries. I don't desire the company of those who get excited about the latest fashion trends, those who know everything about what's going on in the lives of celebrities and or those who talk just for the sake of talking.

I'm hungry for seeking solutions to ending social and racial injustices. I'm thirsty for work, engagements and interactions where I can reach out and emotionally connect with people. I crave magic, meaningful moments, travel experiences and mingling within the various cultures of the world. I want to experience awe and delight in the work I do. I want to see eyes light up with curiosity, smiles as bright as the sun, and lives transform before my eyes. *This is significance.* **This is meaningful. This is magic**!

How much will these moments cost me? How much money do I need to experience all of this marvelousness? Not a lot. Essentially, it's all free!

You don't need a tremendous amount of money to be happy. You don't need money to love and serve people. You don't need money to make a contribution to the world. Experiencing magic and marvelousness in your life *will* cost time and energy. And, I'm willing to invest the time and energy into being love, giving and receiving love, sharing my gifts, serving the world and making a difference. Don't let lack of money or a little money make you miss the meaning and magic you deserve to experience.

It's time for you to unleash your significance, walk in your greatness and be all you are destined to be by doing what you ARE HERE to do! Maybe it's time to stop chasing your purpose, and instead, pause, *remember it* and let it find you. Maybe you're already on the path of your destination and want to pick up the pace. Perhaps you know what you're here to do, and you want to amplify the awesomeness in your life. Where ever you are in your journey, let me offer you an alternative to pause, pick up the pace or amplify your significance.

Instead of struggling to answer the question *"what do I want to do for the rest of my life?"* Answering this question may give you more insight. *How do you want to feel for the rest of your life*? Remember, I talked about how we constantly reach for something to feel or not feel our way through life? THIS is the right moment to reach for that which makes you *feel good* and come alive inside. THIS is the moment to program your *magic button,* so you can push it anytime you need to and experience the magic you seek.

Just like the *easy* button you've seen online or on television, here's your chance to create a magic button just for you! What does a perfect day or moment look like for you? What feelings would you like to feel to experience a magical day? If I were to program my magic button I would infuse it with peace, inspiration, curiosity, creativity, love, deliciousness, gratitude, abundance, vitality, prosperity and meaning. What would you infuse into a perfect day? Use the list below to create your master code for your magic button or add your own to the list. Circle the top ten words that best describe how you want to *feel* every day for the rest of your life.

Creativity	Inspiration	Fantasy
Innovation	Focus	Meaning
Fascination	Glory	Curiosity
Serendipity	Exploration	Love
Vibrancy	Magnetism	Peace
Gratitude	Joy	Abundance
Prosperity	Security	Safety
Laughter	Excitement	Adventure
Compassion	Passion	Faith
Serenity	Purpose	Clarity
Optimism	Determination	Grace
Courage	Bravery	Appreciation
Beauty	Contribution	Satisfaction
Service	Generosity	Empathy
Wisdom	Belief	Happiness
Fun	Connection	Trust
Flow	Synchronicity	Harmony
Intention	Luxury	Truth
Magic	Vitality	Play
Aliveness	Relaxation	Imagination
Confidence	Delight	Leisure
Freedom	Calmness	Authenticity

Which words did you choose? As you continue on your path and evolve to higher levels in life, the words may change and that's okay. Reflect upon the words you chose and ask yourself, "*What do I need and want to do to experience the feelings and experiences associated with these words?*" For example, if you chose the word Authenticity, what does being authentic look and feel like? Does it mean that you speak your mind, dress how you want to dress and or do work where you can just simply be you? Let's say you chose the word Excitement. What activities make you excited? Discover them, and then do more of those activities and or seek out work that is exciting. The ultimate goal is to mindfully and consistently reach for these feelings by doing activities and engaging with people who naturally evoke the feeling.

If you're working a job you don't like just for the money, you have two options. You can find another job that allows you to feel the feelings you desire, or you can seek opportunities within your current job that will allow you to experience your desired feelings. If you are a business owner, it's essential that you stop doing things you don't love just to make money. In fact, once you start truly doing what you love, listening to your soul and using your divine gifts to serve people, you'll bring your business into soul alignment and create more harmony. The joy you feel by really doing work you love will make you more attractive to the clients who crave and want what you are offering. Being love and doing things you love, brings you what you love. It's the *Law of Magnetism*! When you're magnetic, you will also attract more money.

Living a miserable or magical life is *always* a choice. You don't have to wait for the perfect circumstances or until everything in your life is in order. You can start now! You can co-create your ideal life and work with your creator. The purpose path is already laid out before you. It's up to you to choose to walk it as detour and obstacle free as possible. You will make mistakes. You will stumble on the journey. You may lose people. You'll be thrilled and terrified. You may even want to give up and revert back to old ways of thinking and behaving. Don't stop; keep going! Activate the magic within you!

Remember, I told you about the wisdom I received from one of my mentors, Ellie Drake? Well, hopefully you've discovered or chosen what your personal purpose will be. I'm talking about the purpose you have that is *just for you* and no one else. It's important that you live your personal purpose every day. It's equally important to live your *professional purpose* every day to foster meaning in your life. That's what this chapter is about; doing meaningful work in the world.

> Your professional purpose is the work you are created to do that provides you with meaning and money. Your professional purpose is your choice of vocation or career. It's the work you do that provides you with the opportunity to use your skills and be compensated from them.

Note the difference here. Your personal purpose is *just for you*. Your professional purpose is *for you and others*; therefore you give and receive while doing meaningful work. It's also important to note you can accomplish your professional purpose by yourself. You don't need anyone's help to carry out your professional purpose. As you continue reading, and I share more about what your global purpose is, you'll understand *why* I am making *this* distinction. Many people think if they are doing work they love and giving back in their vocation that they are fulfilling their BIG purpose. In some cases, they are; and in many cases they are not. Fulfilling your global purpose has *very little* to do with receiving and that includes money.

It's not enough to just make a lot of money. Creating meaningful money is more fulfilling and will bring you longer lasting joy. Be intentional about how you generate money. Apply for jobs and take positions that will produce the feelings you want to experience. Work for companies that have values you believe in and stand for. Create products, programs and services that are in alignment with your highest values.

> *Do work that feels good, makes you feel alive inside. Do work that inspires and excites you. Do work that makes you leap out of bed in the morning. Do work that is meaningful, magical, brings you money and makes a difference in the world!*

You only get one life; make it count, and make your mark! The world *needs* you and all of your glorious gifts. Don't deny them the opportunity to experience your greatness! Get out your magic belief wand and your magic button and unleash your multi-dimensional magic into the world! Your magic is limitless! Don't hide. **Show up and be magnificent! You matter. You are worthy. You are significant! You can do it marvelous one!**

> *"The greatest good you can do for another is not just share your riches but to reveal to him his own." — Benjamin Disraeli*

I MATTER
I AM
SIGNIFICANT

What is creating misery in your life?

_____
_____
_____
_____

How are you creating misery in your life?

_____
_____
_____
_____

What kind of magic do you want to create now?

_____
_____
_____
_____

What multi-dimensional magic lives within you?

_____
_____
_____
_____

In what ways are you speaking death into your life?

_____

_____

_____

_____

In what ways are you speaking _life_ into your life?

_____

_____

_____

_____

What excites your spirit?

_____

_____

_____

_____

What do you seek?

_____

_____

_____

_____

What do you want to do every day for the rest of your life?

_____

_____

_____

_____

What are you here to do?

_____

_____

_____

_____

What is your true calling?

_____

_____

_____

_____

Describe what a meaningful life would look like for you.

_____

_____

_____

_____

How do you want to feel for the rest of your life?

_____

_____

_____

_____

What will you create with your magic belief wand?

_____

_____

_____

_____

How will you use your multi-dimensional magic to create a meaningful life and change the world?

_____

_____

_____

_____

"Never let your memories be greater than your dreams."

— Doug Ivester

CHAPTER 10

Chapter 10
Be All You Are Destined to Be

ACTIVATE DESTINY

"The only person you are destined to become is the person you decide to be." — Ralph Waldo Emerson

THIS IS IT! It's time. You have another opportunity before you take your last beautiful breath to live the life you are destined to live! It's time to fulfill your purpose, dance with your destiny and truly live and thrive! This is your moment to define and live out your dash, choose your destiny and create your magnificent legacy! I invite you to *be ALL that you are destined to be starting now*. THIS is your wakeup call to waste no more time waiting, wishing and hoping. I invite you to rise, shine, be great and UNLEASH your unique significance! Let's wave your magic belief wand, push your multi-dimensional magic button and activate your greatness!

"Stop acting so small. You are the universe in ecstatic motion." — Rumi

It used to tick me off when I heard people say *"stop acting small,"* and that's because in some ways I knew I was not so much acting small, but definitely *playing* small years ago. And, even today, I know there is a bigger role for me to embody in the world; every day I'm expanding my capacity to carry it. I realized I wasn't playing small in comparison to someone else's way of showing up but, certainly not playing from *my* full potential. By now you should have a better perspective on whether or not you are playing from your full potential. Are you?

When the world was unexpectedly rocked by the passing of Prince (Prince Rogers Nelson), I was surprised by the impact his death had on me. I've always admired his brilliance and musical genius, but I wouldn't say I was an avid fan. The day I heard the news of his sudden death, a somber feeling came over me, and a sense of melancholy lingered in my soul for several days. I watched as the world cried out in disbelief and mourned the loss of one of the great ones. For days, his song *The Beautiful Ones*, stuck in my spirit and occasionally, out of the blue, I would sing a verse or two, and then pause to ponder *why* this particular song attached itself to me. Prince, the *Purple One*, was and is one of the *Beautiful Ones*. He is a G.O.A.T (Greatest Of All Times), and his greatness *transcended* significance. He came. He loved. He served. He transcended and left an everlasting legacy. Prince became ALL he was destined to be!

SAY YES TO YOUR MAGNIFICENCE

Transcendence aka existence beyond the normal level, incomparability, matchlessness, and magnificence is the legacy Prince leaves behind. There will never be another human being who unleashed their pure, magical genius like Prince. Then it hit me. I realized why his death was having such a profound effect on me. What I saw in him, I see in myself. Prince was poetry in motion, a walking wonder, unfiltered authenticity, a lyrical genius, a wise and loving soul, a conscious spirit, a brilliant star in the universe and so much more. No, I will *never* be or be like Prince, yet I too, am all those things in *my* own unique version of splendor and so are you!

It was truly a wakeup call for me to vigorously vibrate at a greater frequency in the world. I've never been inspired by someone's death like this before. And, while I felt sad because of his passing, there was a bigger part of me that was awakened to the true meaning of significance like never before. I knew undoubtedly, that by saying "YES" to unleashing my significance, I had picked up the key to unlock my greatest potential to serve the world generously. I don't write music or play the guitar but words are melodic and my mouth piece (my voice) is my instrument. Prince and I are both messengers with a message that transcends race, gender and class. What is your instrument?

Prince empowered and impacted lives all over the world through music. He encouraged people to love, believe, defy, dare, dream, and celebrate their beauty and uniqueness. That's my message. That's what I am here to do! Prince's passing motivated me to step up, play a bigger role, to fully walk in my greatness and BE significant in all things. I AM THE UNIVERSE IN ECSTATIC MOTION... and so ARE you! We know not when our last day will come. We may take our last breath suddenly. If I were to die today, there would still be dreams, gifts, ideas and desires within me. I refuse to die full. I want to die empty of all my greatness. There's so much more for me to become, to do, to experience, to share and give. I'm *still* full and bursting at the seams to share my significance with the world!

ec·stat·ic: an expression of overwhelming happiness, joyful excitement and self-transcendence.

My man, Prince, surely and ecstatically unleashed *his* significance! What a glorious soul. *Listen up!* You and I have the same potential, greatness and significance within us. Our unleashing will *never* be like his, but we are here to inspire, motivate and empower the world just like him. You may be thinking, how dare I parallel myself to Prince, and my response is confidently, why not? Why not me? Why not you? Prince had a purpose and a calling that he answered and fulfilled. You have that and so do I. At this point in my life, I wake up every day with a throbbing sense of urgency, with an insatiable hunger and thirst for purpose fulfilled. I'm not wasting any more time. I own my greatness whether other people see and honor it or not.

I can hear what my soul whispers to me when I'm all alone. I feel the destiny nudges from the Divine One. I trust the glimpse of greatness that flash before my eyes. I know my creator didn't deposit this dream inside of me to taunt me. God wants me to boldly walk it out. God is beckoning me to be great. God has equipped me with everything I need to manifest his destiny. He's begging me to be magnificent. And to do it all for *his* glory according to his will and my unique purpose and plan. Me, an ordinary woman, who WILL do extraordinary things; that's me. I believe it!

What about you? Do you believe deep down inside of you that you too have greatness, brilliance, genius, giftedness and magnificence? Of course you do, that's why you exist! You're not here, my friend, to just decorate the world with your presence. You're not here to live and then die. You're not here to just survive. You're not settling for what life dishes out; *"you're here to make manifest the Glory of God within you*! (Marianne Williamson)" Do you hear me when I say THE GLORY OF GOD IS WITHIN YOU? I hope you know how awe-mazing you are! There is greatness within you! There is significance within you and now is the time to UNLEASH IT!

Your unleashing will be splendidly different. It won't look or sound like anyone else. This is important for you to believe and digest; otherwise, your ego will talk you out of your brilliance and blessings. You've got to be willing to go into the tunnel of taking your life to the next level with earplugs and blinders on. You must tune out the chatter, gossip, naysayers, Debbie Doubters, and critics and fiercely fine tune your destiny dial to ONLY hear the voice of your creator and your soul. You must commit to not looking to your left or right, behind you or to the grass that appears greener than yours. You got to say "yes" to ferocious focus! **Let the unleashing begin...**

WHAT UNLEASHED SIGNIFICANCE LOOKS LIKE

- Believing that your existence matters. You are valuable. You are worthy.

- Knowing that YOU were created to do something *meaningful* that ONLY you can do.

- Trusting that you were born with a special assignment that ONLY you can carry out.

- Believing you have been given one-of-a-kind gifts, talents, skills and knowledge to carry out your divine assignment.

- Owning your unique purpose in the world and being relentless about fulfilling it.
- Being crystal clear about who you are, what you stand for, what matters, what's important to you and refusing to waste any more time.
- Not caring what other people think of you or worrying about their opinions.
- Refusing to apologize, ask for permission or seek approval to be magnificent.
- Choosing to defy mediocrity, settling and the status quo.
- Fearlessly being love, giving love, sharing love, and receiving love.
- Showing up with unfiltered authenticity and celebrating who you are.
- Living and speaking your truth and playing by your own rules.
- Passionately pursuing your passion and traveling your special destiny path.
- Defining your destiny and doing work you love that makes you come alive inside.
- Discovering the greatness within you and gladly sharing it with the world.
- Being brave enough to create your *own* magic and live a meaningful life.
- Following your bliss and allowing your soul to lead the way.
- Filling your soul cup with what *you need* to fulfill you and serving others from your overflow.
- Joyfully using your divine gifts to inspire, empower and impact the world.
- Making an undeniable difference in the lives of people everywhere you go.

- Being intentional about leaving a legacy that will transform future generations.

- AND EVERYTHING ELSE YOU CHOOSE TO DO WITH AUDACIOUS FLAIR!

I've quoted this powerful passage many times because it's so undeniably true. Even when I examine my own life and observe where I am in this moment and where I intend to be, I too must be reminded of the magnificence within me. I'm not immune to shortcomings, missteps and doubt at times. Every single day of my life I have to remember (because the soul knows) why I cannot quit and that I must go fiercely forward in faith. This passage is perfect when you feel stuck, when you feel tired, and when you feel like shrinking back into average.

"Our deepest fear is not that we are inadequate. Our deepest fear is that we are powerful beyond measure. It is our light, not our darkness that most frightens us. We ask ourselves, Who am I to be brilliant, gorgeous, talented, fabulous? Actually, who are you not to be? You are a child of God. Your playing small does not serve the world. There is nothing enlightened about shrinking so that other people won't feel insecure around you. We are all meant to shine, as children do. We were born to make manifest the glory of God that is within us. It's not just in some of us; it's in everyone. And as we let our own light shine, we unconsciously give other people permission to do the same. As we are liberated from our own fear, our presence automatically liberates others." – Marianne Williamson

I don't know about you, but THIS passage fires me up! – Marianne hit the bull's eye with this brilliant truth. While on this entrepreneurial journey and life, I've come to know that FEAR is one central spirit that has caused the most suffering in my life. I suffered in so many ways I could write a whole other book on fear and suffering. The spirit of fear is powerfully lethal, and it kills more dreams and desires than you can imagine. The spirit of fear shows up in the form of worry, doubt, self-sabotage, regret, and procrastination. Stop for a moment and think of the things you wanted to do or accomplish in life but allowed the spirit of fear to talk you out of them. **Fear is a liar! Fear is a thief! Fear is a dream killer!**

I've heard people say that *if we could see ourselves as God sees us we would not be so afraid, and we'd do greater things in our lifetime.* Wouldn't it be wonderful to see ourselves with the same majestic and loving eyes that God's sees us with? We may never be able to experience that miracle, but we CAN begin to create a panoramic view of all the wondrous gifts we possess. Just think of how far you've come and what you've overcome to be here now. Do you see how brave, strong, and resilient you are? You are a warrior, you are a winner, and you are an overcomer! There's something down inside of your soul that refuses to let you quit – it's the spirit of a champion!

DON'T RUN FROM YOUR DESTINY

The champion within us is what we are more afraid of. The spirit within that is "*powerful beyond measure.*" Our divine light not only may scare us; it frightens and intimidates others. I promise you when you turn up the volume on your divine luminosity you'll hear people say, "*Who do you think you are, you think you're better than everyone, you're too confident, you're stuck on yourself,* and the list goes on and on. Have you heard that before? If not, you are surely dimming your light. I've heard it many times and expect to hear it more often because I AM HERE to make manifest the *Glory of God Within Me.* If you want to unleash your significance, get ready because when you shine in the face of those who dim their light, you'll be talked about.

And, I say SO WHAT! Are you going to succumb to the naysayers and gossipers and forfeit your destiny, or are you going to shine unapologetically and courageously complete your divine assignment? I'm not here to please people and keep them comfortable. I AM HERE to please and glorify God and fulfill my destiny. I'm cool with turning people off, giving them something to talk about and causing them to question their own spirit of fear and champion within. YOU ARE HERE TO SHINE! And, as you do, you unconsciously give other people permission to do the same. As you are liberated from your own fear, your presence automatically liberates others. This is exactly why

Marianne says *"your diming your light does not serve the world."* When you choose NOT to shine it helps keep others in bondage. Your unique light has the divine power to set others free! This is what the world *needs* from you.

I know what it feels like to fear the spirit within that is powerful beyond measure. I've have had several encounters with complete strangers that confirm this spirit lives within me, and that it is more visible to others than it is me. One day I was in the book store, bent down, looking for a particular book on the bottom shelf. Out the corner of my eye to my right, I saw a woman's feet standing still. I noticed her feet and kept looking for the book. Her feet did not move, and I became concerned. I looked up and saw this friendly, yet slightly startled woman staring at me. My concern grew. Her odd presence was making me uncomfortable. She didn't speak or move. She stood there looking directly at me as if I was some strange, yet fascinating creature she'd never seen before.

I finally said, *hello, how are you today?* She said, *I'm great; how are you? I'm doing wonderful just looking for a Louise Hay book called, You Can Heal Your Life,* I replied. *Wow! I'm looking for the same book, isn't that funny,* she said. We chuckled. She still hasn't moved from the original spot she was in. My concern now is a bit unbearable. Something was not right with this woman. She's still standing there looking at me as if she's seen a ghost. I couldn't take it anymore, so I said, *excuse me, but your behavior is odd, and it's concerning me; are you okay?* She said, *absolutely I'm fine, but can I share something with you?* For the first time, she moved towards me without breaking her gaze. *Do you know how powerful you are? Do you know how powerful your energy is lady?* She said.

I really thought this lady was tripping out, but, I was curious as to where she was going with the conversation. *I'm not sure what you're getting at, but I've been told that my energy is powerful before,* I said. *It's powerful beyond description; in fact, so powerful I felt your energy and your presence before I turned down this aisle to see who you were,* she replied. She said she felt my energy as she approached the aisle I was in, and it startled her. My energy caused her to pause, yet proceed to see who in the world was radiating so magnetically. *When I saw you*, she said, *you were just as beautiful and vibrant as your energy felt, and all I could do was stand in awe unable to move.*

I was now motionless and breathless. I didn't know what to say. I was unsure whether to believe her or continue to be concerned about her mental health status. As a trained, seasoned and licensed mental health therapist, I was analyzing and diagnosing this situation from the moment I noticed her paralyzed in place staring at me. My intuition and safety radar were on high alert. She was a typical looking, pleasant woman in her late thirties or so. There was nothing strikingly odd or dangerous about her. I paused for a moment to check in with spirit and silently asked, *God should I be afraid of this woman?* I clearly heard him say, *no; she's just a messenger; listen to what she has to say.*

I relaxed and leaned in to hear more of what she was sharing with me. She went on to tell me again how powerful I am and that I have great, positive, highly vibrational energy. She told me I had divine greatness within me. She told me I was here to do big magnificent work. And then, she stepped back fearfully. She was startled again. Now, by this time, I was saying to myself, *God are your SURE I shouldn't get away from this woman! Be still and listen,* my gut said. I asked her why she jumped back away from me, and she said, "*I know this sounds crazy, and you're not going to believe me but I just saw a big, bright scrolling billboard over your head with flashing lights that said, Genius Saves the World!*"

What the hell? And, as crazy as it sounds, I believed her and feared this truth at the same time. She then touched my chest. I was wearing a t-shirt with the word BELIEVE written in pink letters in support of breast cancer awareness. As she touched the words on my shirt, she said, *you WILL save the world, you are called to do great things but you don't believe it.* She goes on to encourage me to say "yes" to my dreams, to own my energy and to boldly go forth and do my big work in the world. I could feel myself tearing up because this woman spoke LIFE into what I already knew. She confirmed and affirmed the *knowing* I had inside about my divine assignment. And, she was right. I was afraid to step out and just do it.

This woman was a divine messenger. This was no accident; we were meant to have this strange yet familiar encounter. God sent this woman to speak his message in the natural because I doubted my significance in the spiritual. I got my book, paid for it and left the store. I was inspired to move my feet and play at a bigger level. I wasn't completely sure what genius saves the world meant at that time, but I knew I had to turn up the volume of my light and shine brighter. I did that by letting go of many things and people that were distractions from my destiny. My load got lighter, and I became clearer about who I AM and what I am here to be and do.

Has anyone ever spoke life into you this way? Have you had a stranger confirm and affirm the knowing in your soul? Pay close attention to all of your encounters. Be mindful and tuned in because God is speaking to you in limitless spiritual ways. And, he knows that if you're like me, occasionally you need a natural messenger to deeply believe the truth of your destiny. We've already talked about the power of belief, and, if you don't believe in your significance, you won't experience the magnificence of your calling. If you want to BE all that you are destined to be, BELIEVE that you already are!

Being chosen for a unique divine assignment is bittersweet. When God impregnates you with a vision, purpose, dream or assignment you're going want to deliver it and abort it at the same time. You will be delighted and experience moments of doubt. You'll feel terrified and excited. When you're *chosen,* you don't get to only choose the pleasurable moments of your magnificence but you will be required to deal with the pain that comes with walking out your purpose. If you're seeking your destiny and wondering why things may be falling apart or not falling into place, it is part of the plan. Keep believing and faith it forward regardless of what your situation looks like now. Destiny is a choice despite your circumstances.

YOUR TRUEST DESTINY IS CALLING YOU

Let me share one final destiny story for you to emphasize the power of BELIEF. Not too long ago I went to California to speak at a women's travel conference. While the conference attendees were in session, I took a break from my vendor table to explore and support the other business owners in the exhibit hall. It had been a long day, and I decided to get a hand massage from one of the vendors who were promoting reflexology. There were two vendors seated at the massage table, a young man with startling blue eyes and a woman with the most beautiful black curly hair and dazzling smile. For some reason, I was drawn to the woman. I locked eyes with her, smiled and waited for the lady getting a massage to finish.

The woman with the beautiful, black curly hair said, *"Do you want a massage?"* I said "yes" and sat down in her seat. She was a friendly, attractive and happy woman. As she began to rub my hands, she smiled and asked what I do for a living. I told her I was one of the conference speakers, shared what I spoke about and talked a bit about the branding and marketing work I do. I could tell she was listening to my voice but not *necessarily hearing* what I was saying. She listened to the words my voice spoke but was *hearing the message in my soul*. I soon realized this was more than just a hand massage. I could feel it coming.

And then… she said, *"Tell me your name again and can I share something with you?* I told you I knew it was coming, and by it, I mean another divine messenger was about to speak a spiritual message I needed to hear in the natural. She was "reading" my energy. She said, *"Catrice, I felt your energy before you sat down in my chair. Your energy is extremely powerful; almost unbearable. Did you notice that I hurried to finish up the lady before you because I knew I needed to touch you?* Speechless and breathless again, I paused for a moment to really digest what she had just said to me. I then responded to her and said, *"You're not the first person to tell me something like this."* I shared the story I just shared with you about the lady in the book store. She was not surprised by the story at all, in fact, she confirmed everything the bookstore lady had to say.

This divine messenger with the beautiful, black curly hair *spoke life* into my destiny! She told me I have a big cause to champion in the world. She emphatically said that my true calling has nothing or very little to do with branding and marketing. She said, "*Catrice, I know that your current brand-marketing work is filling your bank account, but I also know for certain it is NOT filling your soul.*" She went on to tell me that my greater work in the world will be a solution to the suffering people in the world. When I shared that I believed her and knew that my divine assignment is related to social justice activism, she almost leaped out of her chair. *YES! YES she proclaimed; that's it and specifically your work will be centered on race and women.*

By this time, I wanted to leap out of the chair because I never told her about my last book, *Antagonists, Advocates and Allies* and my recent social and racial justice advocacy work. Finally, she said this to me, "*Catrice, you are meant to speak all over the world. I see you on television, specifically CNN as an expert on social and racial justice issues.*" And, when she said this, I was motionless, breathless and speechless – "*Catrice, you have Oprah Winfrey influence; your work is just as big as hers. Stop what you're doing, and go do the work in your soul now!*" She affirmed with great conviction that vision aligned with my book, *Antagonists, Advocates and Allies* is my divine assignment in the world. I promised her that I would and deeply thanked her for her obedience to deliver the divine message.

I got up from the table and KNEW this moment was the ONE reason I was in California beyond blessing the attendees with an inspirational marketing message. I'm a believer that messengers are always in our presence if we are seeking them and have the courage to receive their message. Whew! My heart was racing, my soul was leaping, I was immensely grateful, I was bubbling with excitement and I was inspired, but I was also anxious. *Oh my gosh*! How does one digest being told they have Oprah Winfrey influence. That is insane! How do you wrap your arm around something so gigantic?

You do it afraid, and you do it like they say about eating an elephant – *one believable bite at a time.* If you don't believe you CAN eat a whole elephant, you won't. If you don't believe when someone tells you that you are talented, fabulous, or gorgeous – you won't feel like it. If you don't believe the dream, vision or desires in your heart will come to pass they won't. If you don't believe your finances will increase exponentially, you'll stay broke. If you don't believe your marriage or relationship will be restored, it will die. If you don't believe you can be healthy, vibrant and free of disease, you will die sick. If you don't believe you can travel the world and feel alive inside, you'll stay home miserable. YOU HAVE GOT TO BELIEVE IT BEFORE YOU SEE IT!

> *"The journey of a thousand miles begins with one step."–Lao Tzu*

I'm not sharing these profound purpose experiences with you to brag. I'm sharing them to walk the talk and show you that even with all of my formal education, degrees, titles, and years of experience; I, too, know how it feels to *know* there is greatness within me and still be humbled by its vastness and anxious about unleashing my unbridled significance. I don't know HOW I'm going to walk out this destiny. I don't always know exactly WHAT to do next. Sometimes I am unsure WHEN to move. WHERE my next step will lead me is undetermined. WHY I MUST step, move and take action is crystal clear and undeniable. Reaching the summit of my destiny seems like a thousand-mile climb, and I will reach the mountain top with one step at a time.

I don't have all the answers and I'm on the journey just like you. However, I do know that in order to do my great work in the world and experience all of the magnificence of God's promises, I must keep moving forward. I know for sure there are two things that will keep me on the path of my purpose and help me arrive at my final destination; exercising the power of my *belief magic wand* and activating my *multi-dimensional magic button*. It's a simple and complex truth; radically believe in the vision, dreams, purpose and destiny God has placed in your heart and use your divine gifts to serve the world. Put that on repeat, and let it play!

HOW TO DISCOVER YOUR GLOBAL PURPOSE

Your service to the world is your global purpose. We've already discussed your personal purpose and your professional purpose. I think your global purpose is a little easier to discover. There is a social problem, a human suffering and or a world crisis that pulls at your heart, makes you weep and calls you to do something about it. Every time you hear about it, whenever you see reports about it on the news or see the fallout on social media, it angers you, frustrates you and you know something must be done to end the pain, suffering or injustice.

These problems, this suffering and crisis impassions you! You can't stand it. You easily climb up on your soapbox and rant about how inhumane or terrible it is. The IT I keep hinting at is the social dis-ease you are here to help cure or eliminate. One defining characteristic of a global purpose is that it is so BIG you'd never be able to accomplish carrying it by yourself. Your global calling will require you to have a team, a network, a community and a tribe to fulfill it. Maybe the social dis-ease you're here to heal, solve or eliminate is poverty, child abuse, domestic violence, racism, sexism, human trafficking or something else that is wreaking havoc in the lives of your worldly brothers and sisters.

Find it. Discover it. Own it. Say "yes" to it. Commit to it and use all of your special gifts, talents and skills to fight a good fight for the sake of humanity. Give your time, money, energy and resources to your global purpose. You'll know it's your global purpose because the thought of tackling this social problem will both excite and overwhelm you. You'll know it's your global purpose when you know you cannot do it alone. You'll know it's your global purpose when you're not even sure that in your lifetime this social dis-ease will die or be eliminated. Your global purpose is a HUGE problem in the world. *It's the elephant in the room.* And, how to you eliminate this elephant size social ill? – *One believable bite at a time.*

You see… you're not different than me or me of you. The reason I feel both delight and dread about my "Oprah Winfrey influence" is because my destiny requires me to carry out my global purpose of eliminating racism and the mental and emotional suffering it creates. Look how long people have been fighting this fight, and it appears as if no one has been fighting to eliminate racism at all. Look at how far we've come as a people, yet the end of racism seems like that thousand mile climb I mentioned before. There is more work to be done. The journey is not over. I know for sure that I must walk the walk one step at a time.

I don't know if I will ever see the end of racism the debilitating psychological effects of this global dis-ease in my lifetime. It doesn't matter. I must join my brothers and sisters in the fight and add my bite to eliminating a social dis-ease that is spiritually and literally murdering people. Together, over time and until we take our last breath, racial justice activists WILL eat that damn elephant! *We must. It's what we're here to do.*

You *must* discover your global purpose and find your brothers and sisters in the fight. Align with them, stand with them and fight a good fight to make the world a better, safer more loving place for humanity. *This is your true destiny!* God created us to love and serve. Fulfilling your global purpose is an *act of love* and is your greatest form of service to mankind. The world needs you and is waiting for you to show up!

The world is full of so much darkness, doom, gloom and despair and for every second that you refuse to shine, you perpetuate the darkness in the world. Refusing to turn on your light makes you a conspirator in the ongoing suffering of the human spirit. Staying afraid and refusing to say "yes" to your global purpose is selfish. It's a dis-service to humanity. Your existence has *never* been about you. It's always been about your contribution to the greater good of humanity. Don't let the world down. *Unleash your significance, walk in your greatness and experience the magnificence of your destiny.*

Guess what? I am on this journey with you. Everything I have shared in this book is true. Every strategy and suggestion I've offered WILL work, but only if you work them. I have mastered most of what I've shared and I'm mastering the others in this very moment. I believe, claim and expect a year from now that my life will be dramatically and deliciously different than it is today. It will be so because I AM doing the work, applying the strategies and using my multi-dimensional magic to create a life that matters, is meaningful and one that makes a difference. I don't sit in a high place ordering you to unleash your significance. I stand beside you, on the purpose journey with you, encouraging you to unleash your significance.

I AM an imperfect perfect, ordinary woman with big dreams who chooses to be GREAT and do extraordinary things. I only get one opportunity to live my life. I choose to make it magical while making my mark. I choose use all of my spiritual gifts and natural talents to fulfill my personal, professional and global purpose. I choose to be light in the world live in such a way that others will re-discover their own light and shine it. When it's all said and done, and when I take my last breath, I will have lived my dreams and fulfilled my destiny on purpose! When I take my last breath I will die empty, yet completely fulfilled. This is my DESTINY DASH to live, and I will show up, shine and do my damn thing... my way. With no regrets!

YOUR BREATHS ARE NUMBERED. *Don't waste any more time.* This is your wakeup call! Your soul knows the way. Listen to it. Choose *right now* to define and live out your destiny dash with zeal, intent and enthusiasm. Choose in this moment to courageously answer *your* call. Unshackle your multi-dimensional magic and whip out your magic belief wand to create your rewarding, remarkable, memorable and magnificent legacy. Don't *ever settle* for less than you were created to experience. It's time! Choose to live fulfilled and die empty. Your destiny is waiting for you to show up! Rise. Shine. Be great. Unleash Your Significance! Be all you are destined to be and use your divine gifts to serve the world! You matter! You are magnificent! You are worthy! YOU ARE SIGNIFICANT!

I MATTER
I AM
SIGNIFICANT

In what ways are you playing small?

_____
_____
_____
_____

You have magnificence within you – what does it look like?

_____
_____
_____
_____

What will your destiny be?

_____
_____
_____
_____

What kind of legacy will you leave behind?

_____
_____
_____
_____

What are your deepest fears?

_____

_____

_____

_____

If you unleashed your true power, what would happen?

_____

_____

_____

_____

What have the messengers in your life told you about your destiny?

_____

_____

_____

_____

What do you need to believe so you can see it?

_____

_____

_____

_____

What is your global purpose?

_____

_____

_____

_____

What will your life be like when you finally unleash your significance?

_____

_____

_____

_____

"You only live once, but if you do it right,

once is enough."

— Mae West

Afterword

You Start Dying Slowly

You start dying slowly
if you do not travel,
if you do not read,
If you do not listen to the sounds of life,
If you do not appreciate yourself.

You start dying slowly
When you kill your self-esteem;
When you do not let others help you.

You start dying slowly
If you become a slave of your habits,
Walking everyday on the same paths…
If you do not change your routine,
If you do not wear different colours
Or you do not speak to those you don't know.

You start dying slowly
If you avoid to feel passion
And their turbulent emotions;
Those which make your eyes glisten
And your heart beat fast.

You start dying slowly
If you do not change your life when you are
not satisfied with your job, or with your love,
If you do not risk what is safe for the uncertain,
If you do not go after a dream,
If you do not allow yourself,
At least once in your lifetime,
To run away from sensible advice…

— By Pablo Neruda

50 Ways to Be More Courageous

[adopted from *The Art of Fear-Free Living: Awaken the Geni(us) Within*]

On the path to fulfilling your purpose the one thing you can count on consistently is fear will show up and try to suffocate or steal your dreams. Every action you take to unleash your significance, fear will creep in and try to convince you to dim your light. On the road to walking in your greatness, fear will be a constant companion called your ego. There is a power within you greater than your ego. It's the hero within. Every day of your life, you must summon your hero and listen to the wisdom of the hero's voice. It will never lead you astray.

The truth about fear is that it will always be a part of your life. The truth about fear is it is most often a future state of mind. The truth about fear is that the best weapon against it is love. The truth about fear is it is powerful beyond measure. The final truth about fear is love of yourself, love of life, love for other people and love for the world can diminish the power of fear and afford you more peace, joy, ease and grace in your life. The truth about you is you can choose to be fearless by living in the now moment; you can choose to love and accept who you are in your core, and you can choose love when fear steps in.

My hope for you is that you begin your journey of truth no matter what it is. It may feel scary, and you may be afraid, but **BE COURAGEOUS IN THE MIDST OF FEAR.** Every step towards fear decreases its power. Every courageous action makes you more fearless. When you are afraid give your energy to this question *"what do I need to conquer this fear,"* instead of becoming paralyzed by the fear. The more resources and support you have as you face your fears increases the courage you'll have to be a fearless champion! When you feel scared, defeated, worried or unmotivated, wake up the champion within and summon your hero to help guide your steps. Here are *50 Ways to Be More Courageous*; use them every day.

1. Make a list of the things you need to forgive yourself for, and one-by-one release the shame, guilt and regret.

2. Identify the people in your life you need to forgive. Choose to do the work within your heart to forgive them.

3. Start a courage journal, and write down all the things you want to do, and find creative ways to make them happen.

4. Choose the risks you can take now to be more courageous.

5. Remember the moments when you were wise and strong and how you were able to create success in those moments.

6. Make a list of the values and standards you want to live by and start living by them.

7. Think about all the things you do that you do not like or want to do and create your "*not to do*" list. Once the list is complete, be brave and just stop doing them.

8. Use your fears to drive you towards your passion and purpose.

9. When you become aware of fear, remember the awareness of fear is a signal that something in your life is missing.

10. See the significance of feeding your soul as you do in feeding your body. Determine how you will feed your soul every day.

11. Check your emotional energy tank, and determine who is filling it or causing you to run on fumes. Determine what you can do to remove the energy stealers in your life and do it.

12. Decide what you can do every day to move from surviving in life to thriving in your life.

13. Every time you feel fearful, ask yourself this question *"what is the worst that could happen if I do not face this fear, and what is the worst that could happen if I do face this fear?"* You'll see you have more to lose by NOT facing your fears.

14. Remember, you only have two choices in life: Be afraid and live afraid or be fearless and live courageous.

15. Instead of focusing your energy on your fears, focus your energy on how you can get the resources you need to conquer the fears.

16. Color the canvas of your life with vibrant, energetic, happy people who can keep you inspired to Master the *Art of Fear-Free Living*.

17. Remember that every day you have the choice to take down the old, dull and grey canvas and put up a blank one to create your fearless life.

18. Know that your personal power is like a big eraser. You have the power and choice to erase the negative thoughts about yourself. Erase the past hurts that are keeping you stuck. Erase everything in your life that is causing you distress and misery.

19. As you begin to create a fear free life, remember that you have the tools you need within you; you just have to seek them and use them.

20. Be mindful to stay off auto-pilot. Be sure to live fully awakened in each moment of your life.

21. Make it a personal priority to ask yourself every day, *"what do I need to face and how can I face it with the resources I need and do it with ease and grace?*

22. Be intentional in every moment. Only engage in activities and conversations that move you one step closer toward your goals.

23. Remember that facing your fears is simply about taking risks. You have to be willing to take some risks to get and experience what you desire.

24. Create a vision board, and fill it up with words, pictures and quotes that depict how you want to live your fearless life.

25. Create your fearless life dream team. A small group of dedicated, positive, trustworthy people who believe in you and your dreams and will help you bring them to life.

26. Be mindful to not make excuses or reasons not to do something that can empower your life. Excuses are the doorway to failure.

27. When faced with a fear, instead of allowing yourself to worry and become paralyzed, seek out the resources to help you conquer the fear.

28. Be curious. When faced with a fear ask yourself this question "*I wonder what would happen if I faced this fear?*" Be still and listen for the answer to come from your heart.

29. Make the choice to accept that you will have obstacles in your life and begin to see them as opportunities to strengthen your hero.

30. Instead of dreading facing your fears, wake up each day with gratitude and ask yourself "how can I be brave today?" And, then take action.

31. *Unsubscribe*! That's right; opt out of everything that does not fill your cup, fulfill you, serve your highest good and or take you one step closer to your highest self.

32. Surrender once a day. In the morning, surrender to the Universe and let God order your steps. In the evening, surrender again and release all the toxicity you've taken in during the day.

33. Choose to be struggle free! Pay attention to the moments where there is struggle and decide in that moment that your life is not worth the pain and frustration that struggle brings.

34. Be accepting. Sometimes you've got to simply say, "it is what it is." Let it go and keep it moving.

35. Quit looking for the answers, and choose to allow them to just come to you, and enjoy life while you wait for the divine downloads to occur.

36. Trust yourself more. Trust that what you need will come. Trust that you know yourself better than anyone else. Stop fighting with your hero and just trust yourself.

37. Take action! Worrying, contemplating, agonizing and analyzing are signs of struggle. Ask your heart and your soul whether you should act, and, if you feel peace overcome you, then get out of your head and take action.

38. Learn how to filter out the background noise. The background noise is other people's opinions, demands and requests. It's your life, do what you want to do, and make your own decisions.

39. Release the need to be right or perfect. There's no such thing as perfect, and you will never be right all the time. Instead, strive to be the best you can be without measuring yourself against anyone and being wrong means you're human.

40. When you stop judging others; you will learn to accept them for who they are; thus you, begin to accept yourself just as you are.

41. Your past is a part of who you are, but it does not determine who you will become. Let go and be free, or keep holding on and be miserable.

42. Take out a new canvas everyday and start over. Yesterday is gone and is a memory. Tomorrow may never come and is a dream. Today is all you have and it is a blessing.

43. Every day you have a choice to stay captive or you can be brave and take out your courage key and unlock your life. Stop wallowing in "what if," and begin basking in your bravery.

44. Look for at least one opportunity each day to grow and evolve. Read a new book, write in your journal; it doesn't matter what it is as long as it takes you one step closer to fearless living.

45. Get over yourself! Someone out there has it worse than you. While you are important indeed, the world does not evolve around you.

46. Fearless living is about survival of the fittest. Either you change, grow and evolve or life will pass you by. Get up, and get into your life.

47. You can't change everything in your life in one choice, but the choice to live fearlessly can dramatically change your life.

48. Choose to live deliciously! Write down your recipe for a delicious life on a real recipe card. Get creative and add in a little spice, passion, excitement, satisfaction and zest and you are sure to whip up a life that makes your mouth water.

49. Clock in and go to work! Living YOUR LIFE fearlessly is an inside job. It's the most important job you will ever work in your life. Go in early, work hard, take on extra projects, be on the leadership team, put in 100%, stay late, clock out and start all over again. When you work this job like it's the only one you'll ever have, the recognition, raises and promotions are guaranteed.

50. *You are the Genie you've been waiting for!* Decide what you want, how you want to be and how you want to live your life and get it, be it and live it. The only thing keeping you from living a rewarding and fulfilling life is you. Tell your ego to get out of the way, and allow your hero to reign in your life. It's your life own it, create it, live it and love it—fearlessly!

If you love these courageous life tips and want to learn in more detail how to live more courageous, order a copy of *The Art of Fear-Free Living: Awaken the Geni(us)Within* at www.bossladyofbranding.com

About the Author
Catrice M. Jackson

The Woman, Healer, Counselor, Entrepreneur, Author, Scholar, Teacher and Contributor

The Woman

Empowering the lives of people is my passion. I embrace the opportunity to blend my rich psychology, counseling, human behavior, social consciousness and leadership skills into messages that make an impact on the human experience and training that transforms consciousness, communities and cultures. I'm on a relentless mission to make a difference and do work that is meaningful and inspire and empower others to do the same. I'm most passionate about social and racial justice because without either, people cannot fully thrive in life and thriving is everyone's right. Everyone deserves to walk in their greatness and live out their purpose without restrictions.

For as long as I can remember, I've always had something to say. I'm often compelled to speak up for the underdog and about the injustices in the world. I'm a humanitarian, a lover of people and soul who is not afraid to talk about difficult topics or have courageous conversations that matter. Conversations that if not engaged in, things stay the same, nothing changes and lives are not transformed.

I value truth, freedom, authenticity, courage and peace and intentionally infuse my core values into every human engagement, keynote speech, training, and workshop and on any platform I am called to be a voice. My style is real, bold, unapologetic, compassionate and playful. My soul intention is to inspire and empower people to take responsibility for their lives, own their personal power and use it to make meaningful changes in their lives and the world. I'm here to be a voice. I'm here to make a difference. I'm here to challenge the status quo, to wake people up into a new, awakened, conscious way of being and living.

The Healer and Counselor

Catrice is a highly skilled Licensed Mental Health Practitioner and Licensed Mental Health Counselor (LMHP, LPC) with 15+ years experience providing intensive mental health counseling service to women, at-risk children and families. She specializes in working with clients who struggle with depression, bi-polar disorder, psychosis, post-traumatic stress disorder addiction disorders, and other cognitive-behavioral challenges. Her preferred intervention and treatment modalities include positive psychology, cognitive-behavioral therapy and humanistic approaches. Catrice is a passionate advocate for mental health awareness and advocacy, and her clients experience rapid therapeutic breakthroughs and life changing results.

The Entrepreneur and Author

Catrice M. Jackson, international empowerment speaker and the truth-telling *BOSSLady of Branding* helps entrepreneurs, business owners and professionals clearly identify their soul-purpose brand and confidently unleash their *Irresistible Trademark* (IT) so they can unapologetically show up in the marketplace, shine and do the damn thing! Catrice is most passionate about helping business owners, professionals and entrepreneurs crank up the volume of their voice to be undeniably seen, heard, loved and hired by clients they crave.

She is a master-message mentor who turns mediocre marketing messages into social media sales succulence, an international speaker who empowers women to step up to the mic, speak their brand and sizzle and loves helping women BOSS their brands by creating a 3-D sensory brand experience clients are hungry for. She does it all with her signature coaching secret-sauce, *Catriceology*, the irresistible psychology of branding anchored in truth, authenticity and freedom. *Catriceology* is uniquely designed to teach business owners, professionals and entrepreneurs the psychology of personal branding, and how to infuse it into their brand-marketing messages to be more magnetic in the marketplace and maximize and monetize their one-of-a-kind, *Billboard Brand*.

Catrice is a two-time international best-selling author, and the author of six personal development and inspired business books. She was a finalist for the 2016 *Author of the Year* by IALA (Indie Author Legacy Awards) for her book *Antagonists, Advocates and Allies*, in the category of Social Consciousness. She has been featured in the *Law of Attraction Magazine* and *Women's Edge Magazine* and has contributed to various online magazines and blogs, such as *Little PINK Book*, *Vivid Life*, *Feminine Soul*, and *She Is Dallas*. She received the *2012 Stiletto Women in Business Award for "Entrepreneur of the Year in Education and Training"* for her dedication and innovative strategies for inspiring and empowering women world-wide. She was named a *Finalist for Woman of the Year for the Unstoppable Woman Conference 2014.*

Catrice's personal mission is to live her truth and evolve into her highest self. Her professional mission is to teach people how to live their authentic personal brand and speak their voice with irresistible confidence on any platform, and her global mission is to liberate the voices of people worldwide so they can live courageously and authentically free. Beyond the titles, products, and programs, Catrice is a God-loving Christian woman, a wife, mother and grandmother. She's a lover of people, a humanitarian, a dreamer, a giver, a doer, a voice for the voiceless and woman who believes everyone should BE in peace by living a life of truth, authenticity, freedom and love and significance.

The Scholar, Teacher and Contributor

Education

PhD— Organizational Psychology, Walden University (In Progress)

- M.S.—Human Services/Counseling, Bellevue University—GPA 3.97
- B.S.—Criminal Justice Administration, Bellevue University—GPA 4.00 (Dean's List)
- Licensed Practical Nurse, Western Iowa Technical Community College
- Certified Domestic Abuse and Sexual Assault Advocate, Trainer and Speaker

www.catriceologyenterprises.com

www.catriceology.com

www.bossladyofbranding.com

CatriceJacksonSpeaks

@catriceology

@catriceology

@catriceology

Made in the USA
San Bernardino, CA
23 August 2017